ELEMENTS
OF
RITE

A Handbook of Liturgical Style

Aidan Kavanagh

ELEMENTS
OF
RITE

A Handbook of Liturgical Style

A PUEBLO BOOK

The Liturgical Press   Collegeville, Minnesota

Design: Frank Kacmarcik

Texts from The Documents of Vatican II
copyright © 1966 The America Press.
All rights reserved.

Copyright © 1982 Pueblo Publishing Company, Inc.
Copyright © 1990 The Order of St. Benedict, Inc.,
Collegeville, Minnesota 56321.
All rights reserved.

ISBN 13: 978-0-8146-6054-6
ISBN 10: 0-8146-6054-1

Printed in the United States of America

Contents

One who worships in spirit and in truth no longer honors the Creator because of his works, but praises him because of himself.

Evagrius of Pontus

Introduction

One thing which afflicted preconciliar Roman Catholicism was a narrow rubricism. Future clergy were usually taught less how to preside at celebrations of the Roman Liturgy than how to confect a sacrament validly and licitly according to the rubrics contained in officially approved liturgical books. The active participation of others in such an act was generally regarded as possible but unnecessary and was discouraged as a distraction of such serious proportions that it was limited to rare occasions. Many parishes thus knew little more than silent low masses as their standard Sunday fare.

Some today argue that in postconciliar Roman Catholicism this malaise has been replaced by another just as grave. It is that of ignoring the rubrics of the reformed Roman Liturgy altogether in the expectation that relevance and good intentions dispense the worshipping assembly and its ministers from rubrical encumbrances. Critics point out that the results of this attitude are evident in declining church attendance, due to alienation of the old and boredom among the young, and in a presumption among some clergy that the liturgy is at bottom an educational opportunity for special groups or therapy for themselves. In attempting to cure a previous malaise, it cannot be ruled out that what has been accomplished is an exchange of one malady for another.

To the extent that there is truth in this, one suspects that the culprit is not a lack of good intentions but a certain naiveté concerning the nature of human ritual in general and of the liturgy in particular. In the *Constitution on the Sacred Liturgy* of the Second Vatican Council two things stand out clearly about the latter. The first is that doing the liturgy ineluctably involves laws or rubrics governing valid and licit celebration. The second is that something more than this is required. "Pastors of souls must . . . realize that, when the liturgy is celebrated, more is required than the mere observance of the laws governing valid and licit celebration" (para. 11). "Yet it would be futile to entertain any hopes of realizing this goal unless the pastors themselves, to begin with, become thoroughly penetrated with the power and spirit of the liturgy, and become masters of it" (para. 14).

One takes this to mean that liturgical laws and rubrics are important primarily because they set a floor beneath which a liturgical act may not fall without endangering its integrity both as ritual in its own right and as an act of that communion of churches known as Roman.

In practice, rubrics are easy enough to discern. They are often printed in red, which is what "rubric" means, or in a special type-face, such as italics, so as to be noticed by those whom they concern. They are included in liturgical books to be helpful in securing a recognizable standard of usage deemed appropriate in worshipping assemblies enjoying each other's communion. To regard them as more than this is usually both unhealthy and unproductive. To regard them as less than this is an attitude which should be watched with care and firmly resisted.

But this book is not about rubrics. It is about what gives rubrics their reason and value. If it cannot avoid occasionally calling attention to them, this is because adequacy of liturgical celebration rests upon them as adequacy of language rests upon rules of grammar. And while grammatical rules alone will not produce great speech any more than liturgical rubrics alone will result in a great act of celebration, neither great speech nor great liturgy can afford to ignore the rules basic to each without risking the collapse of both.

It is not very helpful in this connection to talk too soon about "good" liturgy, especially if the discussion is innocent of the phenomenon of rite in general and ignorant of the criteria which determine what correct observance of the Roman Rite in specific might be. This book means to inform that ignorance, to seduce that innocence. It will attempt to provoke thought by restating some fundamentals rather than by providing recipes. In doing this, it will often use language as an analogy for liturgical usage, both of which are means of communication between people. The equipment with which both operate, moreover, is not the precise signs and concepts of modern science. Nor are language and liturgy ever antiseptic; they have been amply inhabited by us, they wear our smudges and bear our smell. Because they inhale the human condition, language and liturgy change slowly and in similar ways. They are together hostile to being mechanically schematized by computers or to being reduced into sterile systems such as Esperanto.

The analogy may, perhaps, free one from a certain mandarin attitude regarding grammar and rubrics. More importantly, it throws one bodily into history, that thinking of the living and the dead, in John Meagher's phrase, which liberates both speaker and worshipper from revolutionary reductionism and aggression. Despite their occasional usefulness, revolutions always proffer some sort of illiberal idolatry—of the proletariat, of Liberty-Fraternity-Equality, of *laissez-faire*, of community (the Romantic or fascist *Volksgemeinschaft*), of an absolutized devotion. Language and liturgy inculcate a healthy impiety regarding such things because each restrains our rush to believe by recourse to the lessons of history clearly learned. As Winston Churchill, an impious virtuoso of language, said of the English rule of style which forbade concluding a sentence with a preposition, it was something up with which he would not put.

A similar healthy impiety is needed even in regard to some conciliar statements about the liturgy, as when the *Constitution on the Sacred Liturgy* directs that the reformed rites, in order to achieve the distinction of

4

noble simplicity, ". . . should be short, clear, and un-encumbered by useless repetitions" (para. 34). One cannot, however, think in a ritual context of the living and the dead (that is, historically) without soon realizing that human rituals are rarely short, clear, and without repetition. They are more often long, richly ambiguous, and vastly repetitive. This is so because many people participate in them simultaneously. This takes time, requires repetition, and embraces many different facets of meaning the participants bring with them to the act. A liturgy without this time-consuming repetition is one without rhythm; one without rhythm allows little or no active participation; one without participation will communicate little or no crucial meaning. For these very reasons, ritual is a system of symbols rather than of mere signs. Symbols, being roomy, allow many different people to put them on, so to speak, in different ways. Signs do not. Signs are unambiguous because they exist to give precise information. Symbols coax one into a swamp of meaning and require one to frolic in it. Symbol is rarely found among the inactive, the obtuse, the confused, or the dull. Signs are to symbols what infancy is to adulthood, what stem is to flower, and the flowering of maturity takes time.

Another matter raised in the *Constitution on the Sacred Liturgy* which calls for a certain healthy impiety is the statement that ". . . the liturgy is made up of unchangeable elements divinely instituted, and elements subject to change" (para. 21). This, it seems, puts an important truth badly, particularly since the text does little to clarify what these different elements might be. That there is indeed truth in the assertion is suggested by the recognizable continuity of twenty centuries of Christian practice of baptism and eucharist, neither of which Christians have ever had much trouble distinguishing from Saturday bath or Sunday dinner. Yet what the "unchangeable elements divinely instituted" were perceived to be in the rites themselves has not been crystal clear in all churches from the very beginning except, perhaps, for water and oil used in baptism and bread and a cup of wine mixed with water in the eucharist. The Lord is recorded as having told his disciples to go, teach, and baptize, but he did not tell them how to do this liturgically. He is also recorded as having taken bread and cup, blessed and thanked God for them, and then given both to the Twelve with the command to keep on doing this as his *anamnesis*; but he prescribed no rite for so doing. In both instances, the surviving evidence suggests that, if there were an unchangeable element divinely instituted in either, it was less a ritual or verbal element than that the Lord's commands were committed to his hearers to be worked out in practice as their fidelity to him would permit in constantly changing circumstances. The history of Christian liturgy east and west makes clear that this is what they did. His followers were aware that he came not to invent or overhaul a liturgical system but to redeem a world.

It is fidelity to him in his Church, made possible by his grace, that is unchangeable more than a given liturgical act or set of words. All these latter have changed at least to some degree and from the very earliest times, for it is in the very nature of ritual that it is as subject to change as any other mode of human communication. This means that liturgical anarchy is not held at bay by immobilizing certain words or acts. These things live in symbiosis as parts of the whole context of faithful meaning they arise from, serve, and foster. Whether the liturgy changes or not is determined less by individual elements internal to it than by the state of the faithful assembly which celebrates it.

This does not mean that Christian liturgy is merely the whim of a capricious group of people. On the contrary, it means that the liturgy is a most intimate facet of the Christian assembly's lived faith in Jesus Christ and a function of the presence of his life-giving Spirit within it. The liturgy, like the Sabbath, is not a plaything for the faithful assembly but its sustained summons home to God in Christ. It is the fundamental way a church stands before the Father in Christ, filled with his Spirit. The stance is inescapably one of service, of *diakonia*. Thus the nature of the Church assembled determines its liturgy to be *logike latreia*, a discipline or order of service in Spirit and Truth. This discipline or order must be one in which both law and grace are at peace with each other. Should this discipline or order become an arcane abstraction separated from actual liturgical embodiment, liturgical practice, as Alexander Schmemann notes, is surrendered to the mercy of the customs, tastes, and whims of this or that epoch, making it the expression of these tastes and whims but not of the Church in her spiritual and eternal vocation.

This is crucial for liturgical style for two reasons.

First, it puts liturgical laws and rubrics into proper perspective. They are not booby traps of divine wrath meant to go off should the unwary blunder into them, nor the arbitrary products of crazed medieval bishops who cared more about the shape of a miter than about the Gospel of Jesus Christ. Liturgical laws and rubrics are, in John Huels's words, a kind of "liturgical proverb," each containing a grain of truth, but not the whole truth, to be used with discretion and not isolated from others of their kind. They do not all oblige equally—some are really statements of doctrine, others are norms of direction functioning as pastoral guidelines, as explanations of options, or as prescriptions for what must be done. The last say one "must"; the two former say one "may". Taken together, rubrics and laws constitute a checklist of the factors to be considered in the art of putting a liturgy together and celebrating it. Their modesty is important since obedience to them must be tempered by an informed sense of pastoral responsibility to the assembly which is both their subject and object. They must be taken seriously out of respect for the celebrating assembly, not out of an obsession that one or another of them might be discovered at the Last Judgment to have been divinely instituted. Such an obsession paralyzes pastoral responsibility, thus introducing either rigor mortis or a reactive antinomianism into liturgical style. Laws and rubrics then become everything or nothing, and the celebrating assembly will likely succumb to compulsion or mutate into some other sort of entity. Neither is a virtue, and the accomplishment of the Church's mission does not lie in either direction.

Second, grasping the ecclesial context of liturgy is crucial for liturgical style because it puts a premium on pastoral responsibility to the church which worships. This pastoral responsibility rests upon two bodies of knowledge, the first being knowledge about the liturgy itself and the second being knowledge about the state of the assembly which worships. The two are in fact one knowledge in past and present tenses. It cannot remain merely notional, and it must not become idealized because it knows the assembly's past while being part of that past in the present. Since it is knowledge that arises from within the object known, it risks losing its objectivity and grasp on the larger context in which the assembly's liturgical style is practiced throughout the rest of the Church. It is here that the demanding discipline of knowing with a clear-eyed and dispassionate objectivity how the Church has worshipped in the past, and how it must worship now, becomes a crucial quality for liturgical ministers lest local particularity degenerate into idiosyncrasy.

Considerations such as these take one not beyond rubrics but deep into the taproot of their historical and pastoral existence. All the rules, laws, principles, and observations which constitute the following sections of this book are attempts to articulate aspects of this taproot in terms of current Roman liturgical usage. All of them, in turn, rest upon ten affirmations concerning the nature of Christian liturgy itself.

1. Tradition and a certain good order are qualities of Christian liturgical usage (see Rule 1 in the Table of Contents).

2. The liturgy is hierarchically structured (see Rules 2, 3, 4).

3. The liturgy is an act of the Church (see Rule 5).

4. The liturgy requires focal points in space and time which are constant and stable, and which have about them a certain sober splendor (see Rules 6-11).

5. The fundamental criterion against which all liturgical things, words, gestures, and persons are measured is the liturgical assembly (see Rules 12, 13, 14).

6. The liturgy happens in space and time (see Rules 15, 16).

7. The liturgy is neither a text nor an audio-visual aid (see Rules 17, 18).

8. The liturgy forms but does not educate (see Rules 19, 20).

9. Because the liturgy is a species of the genus ritual, it is rhythmic and repetitive (see Rules 21-24).

10. The liturgy assumes the closest correlation between visual, sonic, and kinetic media of expression (see Rules 25-27).

The book's rules, laws, principles and observations are nothing more than implications drawn from these ten affirmations and constitute an informal commentary on them.

At the book's end is a bibliography of some sources and studies which may be found useful for further reading.

Elementary Rules of Liturgical Usage

1. *Avoid disorder and last-minute makeshift.*

The history of Christian worship is a story of flight from disorder and makeshift. Confusion, far more than formality or informality, bespeaks an obscured Gospel and obscures it, as 1 Corinthians 11-14 is at pains to point out. Tradition and a certain good order are qualities of faithful liturgical worship.

2. *Keep the various liturgical ministries clearly distinct.*

That the liturgy is hierarchically structured does not mean that the hierarchy alone do it, but that its doing is the outcome of diverse ministries working in concert for a common end which is never just the liturgical act by itself. The common end for which the diverse liturgical ministries work is not a ceremony but a corporate life in faithful communion with all God's holy people and holy things. For this reason liturgical ministers should never be seen to do in the liturgy what they are not regularly seen to do outside the liturgy.

3. *The liturgical minister must serve the assembly.*

When it gathers, the assembly stands in worship before the Creator as sacrament and servant in Christ of a new-made world. This is serious business. The liturgical minister, being part of the assembly, must think and act accordingly, being neither flippant nor dour, neither informal nor rigid. The minister, especially the one who presides, should know both the assembly and its liturgy so well that his looks, words, and gestures have a confident and easy grace about them. He presides not over the assembly but within it; he does not lead it but serves it; he is the speaker of its house of worship. His decisions must never be gratuitous. They may sometimes be wrong, but they must always be steeped in a sense of reverent pastoral responsibility that is completely infused with the assembly and its tradition of liturgical worship. The sort of ministerial discretion this requires is a high art more important than any rubric ever written—just as the artistry of a good cook is more important to human dining than any recipe ever written.

4. *Ministers must not clericalize the liturgy.*
The liturgy belongs to no one but the Church, Christ's Body, which is both subject and agent of every liturgical act. Since every liturgical act is an ecclesial act, liturgical ministers of whatever order are servants of this act inasmuch as they are servants of the ecclesial assembly. They must, moreover, not only be so but appear to be so. Floods of supernumerary ministers, especially concelebrants, suggest the contrary.

5. *Liturgies for special groups are done rarely and for very special reasons.*

Such liturgies are abnormal because the liturgy is not "for" anyone but the entire Church locally assembled. Abnormal pastoral conditions may indeed necessitate abnormal liturgical activity such as masses in homes or sick rooms or convention centers. Even so, the abnormality of such activity must never be lost sight of, must never set precedent, and must be undertaken only in view of contributing to the normal pastoral and liturgical well-being of the assembly as a whole. When normality is recovered, abnormal practice is discontinued just as special medication is discontinued when health is restored. Ministers and assemblies should beware of liturgical hypochondria and too frequent recourse to special remedies.

6. *The church building is both shelter and setting for the liturgical assembly. Nothing more, but nothing less.*

Liturgical worship happens in space, and space is shaped into place by the meaning people discover within it. Jews and Christians have shaped space into place by discovering that the Creator abides throughout creation. Christians especially can never forget the spatial concreteness an incarnation entails. God did not become a movement, a concept, an ideal, or even a committee, but a man of flesh and bone with a parentage, friends, a language, a country, a home. He inhabited not just a time but places, streets, rooms, countrysides, and by his presence in the flesh he changed them all. The memory of this has never died because his continuing presence by grace, faith, and sacrament still does the same in the world through his Body which is the Church, enfleshed locally in the liturgical assembly.

It goes counter to Christian instinct, therefore, that the place in which the Church assembles should be devoid of all evidence of his presence, or that this presence should be regarded as temporary, capricious, or discrete so as not to restrict him or inconvenience the assembly. He restricted himself by becoming incarnate, and the assembly's only inconvenience is his real absence.

Raw space becomes liturgical place through the change his presence by grace, faith, and sacrament causes. Liturgical place is thus not a monument to the pastor's tastes, or the locale in which the assembly feels most comfortable. Jesus Christ's incarnate presence caused notable discomfort even for those who loved him best, and he is reported to have resorted to violence on one occasion when faced with the obduracy of the temple clergy's tastes. Liturgical place belongs to the assembly only because the space it occupies is first his. He alone makes it a place by specifying its meaning as distinct from all others. To this specification the assembly can only be obedient; for it the assembly can only pray even as it cooperates with him by faith in its specification.

What the church building shelters and gives setting for is the faithful assembly, the Church, in all its rich diversity of orders from catechumen to penitent, from youngest server to eldest bishop. As it meets for worship of the Source and Redeemer of all, the assembly is the fundamental sacrament of God's pleasure in Christ on earth. The eucharistic food and drink are the sacred symbol of this ecclesial reality, which Paul calls simply Christ's Body. Christian instinct has been to house this assembly as elegantly as possible, avoiding tents, bedrooms, and school basements.

The assembly uses its place to do something in. This is the liturgy, by which the assembly celebrates the nuptials of all things with their Creator. Because the celebration outstrips being merely an instruction, a pageant, a meditation, a preachment, or an act of therapy, the assembly as a rule has kept its place open for movement on the part of all. Furniture is used for public purpose and for those who find it difficult to stand or move.

The strong and elemental openness of liturgical place makes for dynamism and interest. It is a vigorous arena for conducting public business in which petitions are heard, contracts entered into, relationships witnessed, orations declaimed, initiations consummated, vows taken, authority exercised, laws promulgated, images venerated, values affirmed, banquets attended, votes cast, the dead waked, the Word deliberated, and parades cheered. It is acoustically sonorous, rarely vacant of sound or motion. It possesses a certain disciplined self-confidence as the center of community life both sacred and secular. It is the Italian piazza, the Roman forum, the Yankee town green, Red Square moved under roof and used for the business of faith. It is not a carpeted bedroom where faith may recline privately with the Sunday papers.

7. *Find the most serviceable places for altar, font, and chair, and leave them there.*

Altars on wheels, fonts that collapse, and presidential chairs that fold away do not free but neuter liturgical place. Since crucial values are perennial rather than disposable, they flock with usage to sustained focal points and thus help to reduce raw space into humane place. Crucial values so incarnated become roots for people's lives. Gymnasia rarely play a profound role in most people's maintenance of a secure identity.

Altar and font normally should be fixed, elemental and powerful in their simplicity, free-standing to allow access from all sides, and worthy of the assembly that surrounds them. The amount of space surrounding each should be scaled to the size of the assembly. Neither altar nor font should be so close to the other as to compete for attention or to confuse each other's purpose, dignity, and quite different kinds of liturgy. The altar is a table to dine upon. The font is a pool to bathe in, a womb to be born from, a tomb to be buried in. Bathing and dining areas are rarely found in the same room, except in churches.

The presidential chair should be modest but not trivial. It is best located not primarily in reference to the altar but to the assembly, perhaps in an opened area in the nave of the church facing both lectern and altar along with the rest of the assembly. This would shift the ceremonial focus of the liturgy, except for the eucharistic prayer, into the midst of the assembly itself, where it seems to belong, given the nature of Christian worship. Outside baptism and the eucharistic banquet strictly so-called, the form this worship normally takes is that of a liturgy of the Word, in which the Word is heard and responded to by the whole assembly, ministers included. Locating the ministerial area and president's chair in the midst of the assembly may thus be the most versatile arrangement.

8. *As its name implies, the lectern is a reading stand rather than a shrine competing with font and altar.*

The shrine of the gospel book is the altar. The shrine of the Gospel itself is the life of the faithful assembly which celebrates the Word liturgically. The gospel book, which is "sacramental" of all this, is constantly in motion, being carried, held, opened, read from, closed and laid rather than left somewhere behind votive lights or under lock and key.

9. *The altar and the baptismal font are the primary spatial foci of the liturgy.*

The altar table is kept free of contraptions such as elaborate bookstands, pots, cruets, plastic things, electrical apparatus, aids to piety, and the efforts of floral decorators. The book of the Word and the sacrament of the Word are adornment enough.

The baptismal area is kept free of rumpled vestments, cotton wads, stacks of reading material, and folding chairs. The pool itself is kept clean. It contains what is called "living water" not because things grow in it but because it moves to give life to those who lie in death's bonds.

10. *Liturgical things are designed for the assembly's purpose.*

The church building houses the assembly. It is neither a museum for ecclesiastical art nor a pious attic. All it contains should possess a sober splendor congruent with the assembly and its sacred intent.

Bread and wine should be just that, not plastic disks and grape juice, not corn chips and lemonade. The assembly uses bread and wine as food and drink in the eucharist. These should be present in form, quality, and quantity to correspond with a banquet's usual liberality, keeping in mind, however, that this banquet's purpose is not to fill bellies but to give thanks to the Source and Redeemer of all things. The eucharist, like the Supper which remains its prototype, fills one with more than food, rejoices hearts with more than wine.

Cups, plates, flagons, and bread boxes should be ample. Cluttering the altar with many small cups is logistically and symbolically inelegant. Use one cup of some significance, together with a clear glass or crystal flagon large enough to fill smaller cups for communion later. The same principle holds for the bread plate: use a single large one from which breads can be transferred to smaller plates for communion later. The eucharist is no more a fast food operation than baptism proceeds from eye-droppers or aerosol cans.

Vestments are sacred garments rather than costumes or billboards. They are meant to designate certain ministers in their liturgical function by clothing creatures in beauty. Their symbolic strength comes not from their decoration but from their texture, form, and color. The basic vestment of major ministers is the stole, which bishops and presbyters wear around the neck and deacons wear over the left shoulder. No other ministers wear stoles in the Roman Rite. Ministers ordained to lesser orders may wear albs. When lay persons carry out liturgical duties it is more fitting that they wear their own clothes as members of the assembly, which is no mean dignity in itself. Dalmatic, chasuble, cope, and miter can be handsome garments and should be worn as compliments to the assembly whose purpose at worship is never merely utilitarian but festive.

Books are means rather than ends. Even so, they should be worthy of the Word they record and of those among whom the Word has taken flesh.

Good images are neither accidents nor fantasies but knowledgeable accomplishments which go beyond what can be observed either now or in time past. As John Meagher says, they are meant to evoke the presence of mysteries the mind has glimpsed, to remind us of the ancestral heritage of worship, to tease us out of mere thought lest we forget that history does not fence in truth, that we may not substitute critical understanding for reverence, that our knowledge is not so complete or accomplished as we often assume, and above all that our memories mix with our longings and our joys to put us in touch with our deepest sense of home.

11. *Churches are not carpeted.*

While rugs and runners may occasionally enhance liturgical place by adding festal color, carpeting in quantity wearies the eye and muffles sound. Even with a good electronic sound system, which is a rarity, a carpeted church often has all the acoustical vigor of an elevator. The ambience of a carpeted church, moreover, is too soft for the liturgy, which needs hardness, sonority, and a certain bracing discomfort much like the Gospel itself. Liturgical ambience must challenge, for one comes to the liturgy to transact the public business of death and life rather than to be tucked in with fables and featherpuffs. The liturgy challenges what Quentin Crisp calls the general notion of Christianity as a consolatory religion, as something nice that Jesus of Nazareth could say to those who turn to him for comfort.

12. *Furniture is significant and kept to a minimum.*

Pews, which entered liturgical place only recently, nail the assembly down, proclaiming that the liturgy is not a common action but a preachment perpetrated upon the seated, an ecclesiastical opera done by virtuosi for a paying audience. Pews distance the congregation, disenfranchise the faithful, and rend the assembly. Filling a church with immoveable pews is similar to placing bleachers directly on a basketball court: it not only interferes with movement but changes the event into something entirely different. Pews are never mentioned in Roman rubrics, nor is there any record that being without pews has ever killed Christians in significant numbers.

13. *Banners are decorative images, not ideological broadsides or opportunities for tricky piety.*

Rather than a festal gesture for the assembly, banners often are a form of disposable ecclesiastical art bearing disposable thoughts which foster a disposable piety. Such banners should be disposed of.

14. *The bearing of liturgical ministers conforms to the scale of the space and the ceremony.*

No sensible person would preside or read a lesson at a liturgy in someone's dining room in the same manner as at a solemn event in a large church. Great spaces and solemn ceremonies require large gestures, different voices, more complex choreography, even different vesture. One who does not sense such things probably cannot be taught them. One who cannot be taught them might consider serving God in solitude rather than in the assembly as one of its liturgical ministers.

15. *Not every liturgical word must be heard by all, but words that need to be heard should be clearly audible.*

Words that need to be heard, and the persons responsible for making them clearly audible, are the following.

President: greetings and invitations
the oration prayers (after the entry, over
    the gifts, after communion)
the homily
the eucharistic prayer
the embolism after the Our Father
blessings

Deacon: directions
litany petitions
the gospel
dismissals

Reader: readings other than the gospel

Cantor/choir: psalm verses of entry, Alleluia, preparation, and communion antiphons
meditation chants

Assembly: acclamations
responses to all greetings and petitions
Gloria
Alleluia
Sanctus
Agnus Dei
Creed
Our Father
Amens

These exhaust the audible parts of the liturgy, and
each part is proper to different liturgical ministers or
to the assembly itself. Blurring the distinctions between who says or sings what is not merely dis-
courteous; it undercuts the enacted diversity of the
Church assembled for worship. This obscures not

only the nature of the liturgy as an act of the entire Church, head and members, but the very nature of the Church itself—a diversified communion of persons with Persons, and a diversified communion of assemblies with each other under the criteria of the Gospel.

16. *The calendar of the liturgical year is to be followed.*
The liturgy happens also in time, and time is shaped by the meaning people discover within it. Jews and Christians have shaped time into a thrust towards an end-time because they discovered this final meaning of time in the self-revelation of time's Creator. The liturgy thus does not sanctify time. Time is a holy creature with which the liturgy puts one in meaningful touch. Once in touch with it as marking the implacable unfolding of divine purpose, one is able to perceive its true nature to be not an endless succession of bare moments but a purposeful thrust home toward its holy Source. Time's sacredness is not imposed by liturgical worship. Liturgical worship discovers that sacredness and summons the assembly to take part in it. This means that the liturgy needs time rather than time needs liturgy.

A calendrical "liturgical year" is the way a particular idiom of Christian faith gives shape to these perceptions. It gives coherent expression to time's meaning. The liturgy is thus never wholly celebrated except over the entirety of its annual cycle, beginning and ending with the re-creational events of *pascha*, Easter. Yet the operational icon of this immense cycle is less the solar year than the creational week, six days of work followed by a sabbath of rest and then the "eighth day" of fulfillment and celebration, Sunday. The Christian cycle is a year of fifty-two such iconic weeks turning upon the full paschal "week of weeks"—the Easter season of seven weeks plus the eschatological fiftieth day of Pentecost ($7 \times 7 = 49 + 1 = 50$).

In view of all this, the liturgy does not passively await an absent eschaton. It celebrates the eschaton's unfolding presence every Sunday, the Lord's resurrection day. For this reason, there is no such thing as "ordinary time" in Christian worship. Nor is Sunday a little Easter; Easter is a Big Sunday, that one Sunday of the fifty-two which follows the day of Christ's work on the cross and his sabbath of rest in the tomb.

17. *"Missalettes" are kept out of the sanctuary.*
The best way to do this is to keep them out of the church building altogether. The healthy assembly with alert ministers should not need the crutch of missalettes. They impede local planning of liturgy. Within the tradition as set forth in the liturgical books themselves, the liturgical worship of a local church must be its own business. Worship options ought not to be preselected in an editorial office removed from the local church and then set down in a printed form less impressive on the whole than a copy of a secular news magazine. Proclaiming the gospel or reciting the eucharistic prayer from such products is never done.

18. *Audio-visual aids, especially moving pictures, are never used in the liturgy.*

The probability of human error or mechanical malfunction in connection with these devices is so high that this alone cautions against their use in liturgical worship. The wrong side of a record, an inverted slide, a broken film or tape all put the assembly's worship at hazard. More fundamentally, however, resorting to electronic devices confuses vastly different types of communication. Ritual activity is a "cool" medium which seduces people into the celebrative freedom of common activity. By comparison, electronic media are "hot" and tend to shove people into corners of passivity or isolation where they are manipulable by unseen wills. For this reason it is difficult to visit or converse with others while a television set is on in the same room. Electronic media, in all their aggressiveness, are better used in unritual contexts for instruction, education, or therapy. To conflate the liturgy with such aids is similar to interrupting a play with recorded reflections, aural or visual, on how the performance is going.

19. *The homily is always on the gospel of the day, and one never preaches unless one has something to say.*

The homily follows directly on the gospel of the day because the former is simply the continuance of the latter by the assembly's president amid his peers in faith. He preaches because he presides in the assembly. What he preaches is the day's gospel as it has assumed form in his own life of ministry in the assembly. It is Good News to which all have access and which all have lived, a painfully familiar given. The assembly's president thus does not preach the unknown to the unknowing. Rather, the president's homily witnesses and celebrates the already known and lived which constitutes his assembly and defines his own service therein. If he finds this radically impossible, then it must be questioned whether he is not dealing with a mere audience rather than a faithful assembly, and whether in such a case the liturgy can be more than dissimulated.

Far from being merely an instruction or a religious talk, the homily is an act inherent to the rhythmic ritual of the liturgy. The homily must therefore be soaked with the gospel in its liturgical context. It is never just an act of technical exegesis or a few words of uplift which takes place during a break in the service.

If the president of the assembly is incapable of a homily in its liturgical context, it would be better for him to keep quiet and allow the gospel reading to stand by itself, which it is usually always able to do. Homilists who preach poorly do so as a rule not because they are inept at public speaking, but because they have nothing to say about the gospel worshipfully perceived. For such persons the homily is a problem rather than an opportunity to hear the gospel out loud, so to speak, amid their peers in faith.

20. *The liturgy is never used for ulterior motives such as education.*

Being, like the feast, an end in itself, the liturgy inevitably forms its participants but does not educate them in the modern, didactic, sense of the word. Other media and contexts are available for education. Conflating liturgy and education produces poor education and dissimulated liturgy. The liturgy, like the feast, exists not to educate but to seduce people into participating in common activity of the highest order, where one is freed to learn things which cannot be taught.

21. *Repetition and rhythm in the liturgy are to be fostered.*

No rule is more frequently violated by the highly educated and well-meaning, who seem to think that never having to repeat anything is a mark of effective communication. Yet rhythm, which organizes repetition, makes things memorable, as in music, poetry, rhetoric, architecture, and the plastic arts no less than in liturgical worship. Rhythm constantly insinuates, as propagandists know. It constantly reasserts, as good teachers know. It constantly forms individuals into units, as demagogues and cheerleaders know. It both shrouds and bares meaning which escapes mere words, as poets know. It fuses people to their values and forges them to common purpose, as orators such as Cato, Churchill, and Martin Luther King knew. It frees from sound and offers vision for those who yearn for it, as the preacher of the Sermon on the Mount knew. Liturgical ministers who are irreparably arhythmic should be restrained from ministering in the liturgy.

22. *Words and ceremonies overlap like shingles on a roof; they entwine like vines on a wall, themes in a fugue.*

A liturgical event is not a series of separate tableaux but a symphony of sights, sounds, gestures, and movements whose whole is greater than its parts. The parts must therefore be intimately articulated and the whole well calibrated toward its main purpose. Barren silences, during which one must watch some minor ceremony such as the deacon being blessed before he reads the gospel, disrupt calibration, squander rhythm, distract the assembly, and frustrate the relation of one liturgical part to the greater whole. A symphony is not performed as a series of instrumental solos.

Rhythmic calibration of a liturgy's parts must be a central concern of the president and his deacon. It is one crucial way in which they fulfill their pastoral responsibility for the assembly's worship. This pastoral responsibility transcends individual rubrics. "Pastors of souls must . . . realize that, when the liturgy is celebrated, more is required than the mere observance of the laws governing valid and licit celebration" (*Constitution on the Sacred Liturgy*, para. 11).

A case in point is the rubrically required penitential office between entry and Gloria. This office, which is usually a wordy and prosaic recitation, frustrates rhythmic calibration when, on more festive occasions, an entry procession with chants or hymns cannot flow directly into a solemn incensation of the altar and the Gloria. In such a situation, pastoral responsibility for worship, recognizing the need for rhythmic calibration of liturgical parts, would insist either that the penitential office take the form of a sung litany with *Kyrie* response, or that the penitential office on this occasion be omitted altogether—lest the liturgical action at this point fail the assembly's festive purpose.

23. *Liturgy must never take on a tentative or dubious air.*

A tentative, dubious, or periphrastic feast is a symptom of something's being amiss in the assembly which celebrates it. If such is the case, the feast should be cancelled or deferred until the assembly becomes capable of its celebration once more. The alternative is to dissimulate the feast and thus compound the original problem, which always lies beyond the power of the festal celebration alone to correct. A harvest festival will not make crop failure go away. Here, the problem lies not on the festal table but in the fields and among those who work them.

The moral in this for liturgical celebration is as hard as it is unavoidable. The celebration may well be impossible because repentance has not been undertaken, penance done, or conversion consummated. These endeavors, which are acts of worship in their own way, represent the sort of effort in faith which makes all festal celebration, liturgical or otherwise, possible. For Christians can never forget that they are a free people who have constant access to forgiveness in Christ. They thus are capable of celebrating all things, save sin, in the same joy and confidence with which they were redeemed by the triumph of the cross of Christ. It is for this reason that the assembly is always wary of fantasy but never debilitated by guilt, clear-eyed about itself but never without joy, never confident in its own strength but always assured of God's justice and mercy. To hold otherwise is for the assembly to have followed some light other than that of the Gospel.

24. *To be consumed with worry over making a liturgical mistake is the greatest mistake of all.*

Reverence is a virtue, not a neurosis, and God can take care of himself.

25. *One sings at celebrations.*

Singing is normal when people have something to sing about. They usually do not sing about their sins, but it is hard to stop them singing about forgiveness and reconciliation, the overtures to celebration. Clergy and people stopped singing at the liturgy in direct ratio to casuistry's gradual clarification of how many were the ways one could sin in church. The general expectation that liturgical ministers should be able to sing as one condition for their being ordained then lapsed. And there was a great unwholesome silence in the world which was not without evangelical and theological significance.

While one can bear a liturgical president who cannot preach since there is always the gospel to fall back

on, and while a singing bishop is usually a cross that
need be borne infrequently, a deacon who sings
badly or a president who does not even bother are
afflictions none can avoid. A deacon who cannot sing
is like a reader who cannot read, a presbyter (which
means elder) without age or wisdom, a bishop
(which means overseer) who cannot see, a president
who cannot preside.

26. *Choir and cantor are servants of the assembly, not
surrogates for it.*

The human voice is the premier musical instrument
in liturgical worship, and its basic repertoire is the
psalms. Mechanical devices are secondary at best,
and their various repertoires are frequently tangential
to the assembly's liturgical purpose. This is a hard
saying which needs frequent repetition. For as liturgical worship is not an educational endeavor it is also
not an esthetic event. This does not mean that liturgy
does not form its participants any more than it means
that liturgical worship should be ugly. It means only
what it says, that educational or esthetic fixes are not
what liturgical worship is about. If one goes to
liturgy for a discussion of current events or the latest
ideology, one goes for the wrong reason. If one goes
to liturgy for the organ prelude or choral anthem, one
goes for the wrong reason. And once wrong reasons
invade liturgy, or anything else for that matter, there
is no end to it. For then all mutates into something
else; liturgy becomes a lecture, worship little more
than a crutch for culture rather than critic of its de-
fects or excesses.

Cantor, choir, and instrumentalists minister to and support Christians singing, serving the assembly before they serve their professions. Where possible, they should be placed at the liturgy so that their service to all is as obvious and effective as the services of lector, deacon, server, and president. As the president's liturgical book is the sacramentary, as the deacon's book is the four gospels, as the lector's book is the lectionary, so the choir's and cantor's book is the psalter.

27. *Solo dance performances in the liturgy are to be avoided.*

The liturgy itself is a complex and solemn form of communal dance, of formal motion the choreography of which is its ceremony. If one wishes to enhance the assembly's appreciation of bodily motion as a means of expressing and communicating sacred values, one might give attention to the liturgy's ceremonial choreography and to freeing the assembly from the physical restraints pews force upon it. The introduction of soloists who dance "for" the assembly often has the effect of reenforcing the assembly's passivity by presenting it with a virtuosity of movement none but the soloist can attain.

While such dance events are often exhilarating to many, they are always liturgically superficial. It may help to remember that cultures which retain strong traditions of folk dancing rarely if ever dance in church, but they invariably assign greater significance to ceremonial participation in the liturgy on the part of all. They also tend to keep their liturgical places free of immoveable pews. The liturgy assumes the closest relationship between visual, sonic, and kinetic media.

Some General Laws of Liturgy

1. *Because liturgy is a complex act in which many people participate in many different ways, it is by nature conservative and resistive to change.*

It is often mistakenly assumed that the liturgy is conservative because the Church is a conservative entity which by nature supports whatever status quo happens to be at hand. But whether or not the Church at large is this way (and it is not always found to be so), its liturgy remains by nature conservative and resistive to change. This is due less to theological than social reasons. For when change occurs in group behavior, participation is jeopardized, as those who play games and the leaders of organized sports know. Ritual systems such as the liturgy do change, of course, but the change which is appropriate to them is the result of extremely long-term processes generated within those systems by the people who create and use them. This sort of change enhances participation rather than jeopardizes it because it is generated among the participants themselves, and its course is so subtle that it is rarely remarked upon. The change which all ritual systems resist is external change prosecuted too rapidly and in too great quantity.

2. *At times of high religious intensity in particular, liturgy tends to retain archaic structures.*

This law is social and anthropological, having to do not with arcane theological interpretations but with the religious sensibilities of the liturgy's participants. An example pointed out by Anton Baumstark, who first enunciated the law, is the Roman Rite's observance of Good Friday. On this day of highest religious intensity, the Roman Rite retains the archaic usage of celebrating no eucharist except on Sunday. The Good Friday liturgy to this day takes the form of a service of readings, intercessions in the form of the old Roman solemn "Prayers of the Faithful," and communion from the reserved Sacrament—to which the later, and alien, veneration of the cross has been added. Other examples might be Methodists who sometimes use the "Covenant Service" of Wesley on days of special significance, and Lutherans who sometimes use Luther's *Deutsche Messe* in a similar manner.

3. *Psalmody, which is native in Jewish and Christian liturgical worship, recedes as composed music expands.*

The psalter was for centuries the liturgy's only hymnal because it was thought that the liturgy should consist solely in the celebration of God's Word in both written text and incarnational fulfillment. The liturgy was not viewed as scripture's step-child but as scripture's home. Musical hypertrophy, perhaps as much as any other factor, has been responsible for introducing tension between scripture and liturgy, rendering the relationship between all three problematic.

Many Church Fathers were aware of this early on, cautioning the churches about the power of virtuoso music to distract from the assembly's liturgical purpose.

4. *The Roman Liturgy tends to resist metrical hymnody except in its liturgy of the hours.*

With the exception of several metrical sequences of relatively recent date, the Roman eucharist has never contained metrical hymns. Although these are now frequently included in eucharistic liturgies, especially in northern European cultures which have rich traditions of such hymns stemming from non-Roman sources, the older pattern of antiphon with psalmody remains the preeminent norm in standard Roman eucharistic books. Unfortunately, the current English translations of these books make it difficult to observe this Roman tradition, except for the meditation chants between the lessons.

5. *As the kinetic arts of ceremony decline in the liturgy, the sonic arts of liturgical oratory and music change in nature or disappear altogether.*

This suggests that there is a psycho-social link between the rhythms of movement and sound, and that the rhythm of movement is prior to the rhythm of sound. Hence it may be profitable to consider the effects which the immobilization of the assembly, caused by the proliferation of pews, has had on liturgical speech (the modes of prayer and declamation) and on liturgical music once these are allowed to develop without fundamental reference to ceremonial movement. Liturgical speech then functions less to organize and direct a public assembly toward its common and objective purpose; it functions more to address individuals sitting in place and having the leisure to reflect on their own subjectivity. Liturgical music then functions as a set-piece for appreciation by intently listening audiences, and textual meaning becomes overshadowed by compositional and performative virtuosity; it is no longer music to move by—"parade" music, simple and rhythmic—but music to listen to.

6. *Since liturgical ministry is a service function, its existence corresponds to need.*

Liturgical ministers are ordained, commissioned, or designated to serve their assembly's needs. Liturgical ministries are therefore not dispensed as an honor, nor are they proliferated without reference to need. The law, however, implies more than this because the service liturgical ministry renders the assembly goes beyond the specific function a given ministry regularly performs in the liturgy. While the reader, for example, serves the assembly by reading a lesson, he or she thereby serves the assembly even beyond the time of worship by having placed before it the living example of one who is palpably and publicly concerned with God's Word. The reader is someone who not only reads texts in public but embodies the Word for the assembly's benefit.

A liturgical minister of whatever order thus performs the service which he or she has "become" as an enfleshed sacrament of some aspect of the ministerial nature of the assembly itself. In the liturgical servant this ministerial nature of the assembly takes on personal form in a human scale that is regularly accessible to every member of the assembly throughout the year. Ministers make ministry concrete both in their function and in their own life. Quality of function and quality of life cannot be separated in the liturgical minister without disservice to the assembly. The assembly is not well served by ten vested readers who read two lessons badly, by four cantors who cannot sing, by a dozen deacons too proud to serve or too slothful to learn, by a president who cannot preside.

The connection between the quality of ministerial function and ministerial life is not achieved automatically by ordination, commissioning, or designation. It is achieved under grace by constant prayer, reflection, self-discipline, and continuing practice on the minister's part. This amounts to a fairly high sort of asceticism no less rigorous than that which secular audiences expect of musicians, scholars, dancers, and athletes. For this reason the Church has often gone to its ascetics as one source for its major liturgical minister, the bishop, whose relationship to his assembly of assemblies (or diocese) it has spoken of as an indissoluble marriage bond. In this view, the increasingly frequent practice of what, with reluctance, might be called episcopal serial polygamy, together with enforced retirement of bishops at a certain age, cannot but undercut the enfleshed sacramentality of episcopal ministry in favor of emphasizing its functional duties. The analogy of ministerial espousal in service to the assembly shifts to a paradigm of bureaucratic administration of the local outfit, a shift one has every reason to deplore.

While liturgical ministry is basically a function of service, it presumes that the minister both appears to be and is in fact a servant of the entire ecclesial communion of service. If the Body of Christ is anything it is, in Pauline terms, the nuptials of God and man in Christ, a grand ministry of reconciliation of all to God in Christ.

7. *Liturgy is essentially antistructural.*

Since liturgy is a complex mode of divine and human communication, and must therefore draw upon human structures for all its elements of expression, it is easy to overlook or to forget the fact that liturgy, like ritual in general, exists to undercut and overthrow the very structures it uses. This is so not because the Gospel is similarly antistructural, which it is, but because historic human wisdom has detected that human structures ossify and become oppressive or disintegrate when left to themselves. Bureaucrats and their bureaucracies implacably become tyrants and tyrannies when they are not regularly undercut, overturned, or reversed. This can be done by revolutionary violence, which is usually traumatic for the social group as a whole. Or it can be done more gently and regularly by irony and ridicule, as in a Saturnalia or Feast of Fools in which the structures of the social group are reversed, the high are brought low, and a certain salutary chaos is allowed free rein for a certain well-defined, well-protected time. This works to the good of the social group by restoring its necessary structures after having put them all "in their place." The lesson human wisdom seems to have learned is that although we probably cannot do without bureaucrats and bureaucracies, we certainly can do without tyrants and tyrannies. Ritual and liturgical antistructuralism, therefore, exists not to destroy but to renovate social structures, and it does this not as an end in itself but in service to the general social good.

One important way ritual and liturgical antistructuralism accomplishes this is by recourse to archaism (see Law 2). The archaic is not the obsolete; it is to the human story what the unconscious is to the human psyche. Tapping the archaic is to release unrecognized reservoirs of memory, the power of which may well be as overwhelming as it is difficult to control. But it is power still, and nothing less than power of such dangerous magnitude is required when human structures are to be undercut, overturned, and reversed in favor of social survival. The liturgy exists to conjure such power and to channel it into points of incandescent intensity for the life of the world. For this reason the liturgy especially resists that sort of change (see Law 1) which would so adapt it to contemporary culture as to make it seem indistinguishable from a meeting of the PTA or a political caucus. For this same reason those who hanker after Latin or the English of the Authorised Version should not be dismissed as lightly as some have done. Christian worship, it must not be forgotten, is deep *anamnesis*, remembering. It exists to tap the power of the assembly's memory about events, words, persons, and deeds which jerked the world definitively onto new courses, to conjure that power in the present where it confronts nothing less than the powers resistive to such new courses—the powers of death and darkness, which do not accept being undercut, overturned, or reversed gladly.

8. *Discipline breaks down and accretion occurs most often at the beginning and end of liturgical events.*

Entries and exits are by nature "soft" parts of any liturgical service where some confusion and improvisation are always involved. For what seems to be precisely this reason, liturgical experts and ecclesiastical authorities have pounced upon these two moments as ideal times in which to add various elements to the standard service, often to the detriment of the event as a whole. It is to the beginning of the eucharistic liturgy that the Byzantine Churches transferred the preparation of gifts (the prothesis) and the Prayers of the Faithful (the *Irenike* or Great Synapte litany), thus leaving gaps elsewhere in the service which lead to warps in practice and piety. It is to the beginning and end of the eucharistic liturgy that the Roman Churches added offices of ministerial preparation (the old "Prayers at the Foot of the Altar"), hymns such as the Gloria, the old "Last Gospel" from the prologue to John, and the "Leonine Prayers" mandated by a modern pope against, among other things, Masonic influence in European Catholic life at the end of the nineteenth century. The latter two were done away with by the Second Vatican Council, but the former remain, now transferred into the standard order of service as the "penitential rite" where, with the Gloria, the two continue to confuse the pastoral and liturgical symmetry of the Roman rite of entrance.

9. *The liturgy is not a single service but a complex of services which structures the Lord's Day from beginning to end.*

The notion that the only service needed for observance of Sunday is the eucharist is a notion not much older than the present generation. Within living memory many parishes, even in the United States, maintained the tradition of celebrating at least some of the liturgy of the hours, especially Vespers, in addition to the eucharist on Sundays. This reflected, at least vestigially, the deeply rooted Christian practice of setting the eucharist firmly in the midst of a rich solemnization of God's Word, particularly on the day of the incarnate Word's resurrection from the dead. The eucharist was thus perceived to be the central, but by no means the only, liturgical event lending form and meaning to that one day of the week which was iconic of the whole of a redeemed order in space and time. Paradoxically, the Second Vatican Council's emphasis on the dignity of God's Word seems not to have been translated into reformed liturgical practice, except in the addition of a third lesson to the reading service of the eucharist. When it comes to the liturgy of the hours, the conciliar reform concentrated on reforming the clergy's breviary without carrying this into the area of common prayer for the assembly as a whole. The effects of this on Christian perception of the Sunday, and on perception of the eucharist in context of rich celebrations of the Word on that day, have been less than helpful for evangelization, catechesis, and healthy church order. For the fundamental Christian feast is the Sunday, and it is celebrated liturgically by the assembly's steeping itself in the risen Word heard and sacramentally received as food and drink.

10. *Liturgy is not fundamentally prayer but rite.*

Not every prayer is liturgical, but rite always includes prayer without being reducible to this form of discourse alone. Rite means more than liturgical customs. It could be called a whole style of Christian life, which is to be found in the myriad particularities of worship, in canonical law, in ascetical and monastic structures, in evangelical and catechetical endeavors, and in particular ways of theological reflection. The liturgy specifies all these, and in doing so makes them accessible to the community which assembles within a particular style of Christian life. This is why the liturgy outstrips being reduced to prayer alone, as its several parts demonstrate. Creed and homily are not prayers but declamations; Sanctus and Agnus Dei are not prayers but acclamations; lessons and gospels are not prayers but proclamations. Traditionally, there are only three groups of public prayers in the Roman eucharistic rite: the three "orations," the Prayers of the Faithful, and the great eucharistic prayer. All other prayers are later and more private in nature, and everything else is something different.

11. *The liturgical assembly is less a gathering of individuals than a dynamic coordination of orders.*

These orders are catechumens, servers, penitents, deacons, the baptized faithful, presbyters, and bishops. Each of these groups, in transacting their own business both in and out of the liturgy, contributes to the consummation of the business of the whole assembly both in and out of the liturgy. The assembly enacts itself publicly by order, for Christians differ by groups in their relation to the Gospel. Thus their shared witness, charisms, obligations, and styles all contribute in rich diversity to the Church's ministry of reconciliation. It is a central part of the pastoral art to be able to discern, respect, and coordinate the rich gifts of these orders both in and out of the liturgy for the good of the Church and the world to which the Church is corporate minister by God's grace.

12. *The Sunday liturgy of Christians addresses itself primarily to the object of the assembly's ministry, the world.*

The Sunday liturgy is not the Church assembled to address itself. The liturgy thus does not cater to the assembly. It summons the assembly to enact itself publicly for the life of the world. Nor does this take place as a dialogue with the world, often a partner whose uninterested absence reduces the dialogue to an ecclesiastical monologue. The liturgy presumes that the world is always present in the summoned assembly, which although not of "this world" lives deep in its midst as the corporate agent, under God in Christ, of its salvation. In this view, the liturgical assembly *is* the world being renovated according to the divine pleasure—not as patient being passively worked upon but as active agent faithfully cooperating in its own rehabilitation. What one witnesses in the liturgy is the world being done as the world's Creator and Redeemer will the world to be done. The liturgy does the world and does it at its very center, for it is here that the world's malaise and its cure well up together, inextricably entwined.

Principles for Putting Liturgy Together

1. *A liturgical event, like a sentence, contains parts which function in different ways. It also belongs to units larger than itself.*

As a writer must know the nature and function of the various parts of speech, so one who is responsible for putting a liturgy together must know its parts and their different functions. A liturgy is neither a monolith nor a univocity, but a functioning concert of parts done by different persons. The way these various parts combine constitutes the grammar and syntax of rite in a particular liturgical idiom. And while liturgical parts are for the most part common across Christianity, the ways in which they are used vary widely, producing distinct idioms such as the Syrian, Byzantine, Egyptian, Gallican, and Roman. To study the various Christian liturgies comparatively is to study dialects of a common liturgical language, a study which often sheds light on one's own.

The main *verbal* parts used in the liturgy are the following.

Prayers: petitionary orations, such as the entry prayer, prayer over the gifts, and communion prayer.
intercessions, such as occur sequentially in litanies.

praeconia, such as Easter *Exultet*, which are
unmetered prayers highly rhetorical, even
poetic, in nature.

apologiae, such as the acknowledgements of
unworthiness in the president's private
prayers at communion. These are never
said aloud.

thanksgiving prayers, the most important
of which is the great eucharistic prayer of
the president over bread and wine. This
prayer has evolved into a continuous pro-
clamatory declamation of *anamnesis*-thanks-
giving and is proper to the president alone.

Acclama-
tions: such as "Christ is risen . . . ," Alleluia, and Agnus Dei. These are
short, simple, and easily memorized,
affording the assembly opportunities
to participate frequently in verbal ut-
terances of president, deacon, reader,
cantor and choir.

Hymns: unmetered, such as scriptural canticles,
Sanctus, and Gloria; metered, such as sequences, office hymns, and the like. Unmetered hymns, especially those of some
length, are sometimes difficult for the assembly at large without some assistance
from cantor or choir.

Psalmody: predominant especially in the liturgy of
the hours, but also in the eucharist at entry, preparation, communion processions
and between the readings as meditative

chants and with Alleluia before the gospel. The same difficulty occurs with psalmody as with unmetered hymns on the assembly's part. For this reason, tradition associates antiphons with psalmody—short phrases the assembly can easily repeat between verses sung by cantor or choir similar to acclamations.

Lessons: which the liturgy presumes are always from God's Word or, in the liturgy of the hours, sometimes from approved works which lie close to God's Word, the liturgy being fundamentally the celebration of that Word and no other.

Blessings and consecrations: which are graceful gestures and words meant to recall the assembly to him from whom all good flows. The assembly is aware that neither it nor any of its ministers make things holy. Things and persons are holy just as creatures of an all holy Creator. All the assembly and its ministers can do is to discover and proclaim that holiness to the most intense degree which seems appropriate to the occasion.

Invitations, dialogues, responses, greetings: which are the stylized form taken by the discourse necessary for transacting public business in faith.

Dismissals: originally these were several, especially in the eucharist, complex in form and thus rather protracted. Most occurred at the end of the service of readings, when catechumens, penitents, and the "possessed" were dismissed from the service with common prayers, a blessing, and dismissal of each group in sequence—a mark of the assembly's pastoral concern for each group in its midst who were not considered capable of doing the eucharistic banquet, at least for the present. So important a service were the dismissals thought to be that the Latin churches came to refer to the entire eucharistic rite as *missa*, the dismissal. The dismissal of catechumens has been restored in the Roman liturgy by the 1972 *Rite of Christian Initiation of Adults*. While no specific procedure is prescribed for such a dismissal, the tradition suggests that some sensitive form for doing this must be developed.

Litanies: which are a longer or shorter sequence of brief petitions or intercessions. These occur in both liturgies of the hours and the eucharist, and in addition during processions of various kinds.

Homilies: these are creative opportunities for the assembly's president to retell and give specific point to the gospel within the liturgy.

The homily must be sensitive to its being a part of the liturgy rather than time out from it. The homily must not separate Word and sacrament but unite them. It does this by speaking of the Word not academically but parabolically as the Lord did—in story, sign, symbol, image. These are models of discourse sympathetic with the liturgy, which enacts the Word in the same ways. The homily is not a religious, political, or devotional talk. It is an intrinsic part of the liturgy and must be governed by liturgical laws and principles.

The main *nonverbal* parts used in the liturgy are the following.

Silence: this is not the embarrassed, barren, uncontrolled lack of sound which occurs when things break down and no one knows what to say or do. Liturgical silence is purposeful, pregnant, and controlled—the thunderous quiet of people communicating that which escapes being put into mere words. Such silences should be allowed for after lessons well read, after homilies well preached, during communion time and after it, and at any other unexpected time when silence seems to speak louder than words or music. Such silences should not seem to interrupt the rhythm of the service but to be an integral part of that rhythm.

Processions: moving together, even vicariously as at a parade, is a compelling human experience because of the solidarity with others which rhythmic and coordinated movement seems to make palpable. The key is coordinated rhythm of motion, speech, and music, all of which are best kept simple and repetitive so as to foster participation by making recourse to books and other printed materials unnecessary. Processions, whether penitential or festive, also need elements of ritual and artistic flair, as one so often sees in secular parades, trooping of colors, and even funeral corteges. In most churches processions are usually perfunctory, ill-planned, poorly executed, arhythmic, and utilitarian at best, characteristics foreign to a good parade or procession.

Gestures: these are body-language acts of communication within the assembly. They should have the naturalness appropriate to such communication and avoid seeming bizarre, overwrought, precious, or humdrum.

Sounds: not all sounds are verbal sounds. Melismatic chant concentrates not on words but on the sheer splendor of melody, and the same applies to good instrumental music and to the pealing of bells. Non-verbal sounds are important components of liturgical worship to which too little thought is given. They help reduce the verbosity of liturgy done by ministers and assemblies who assume that liturgy is a text and that celebration requires continual talk.

Sights: while the liturgy is not a stage show nor its ministers actors, the entire event is something which is not only said but seen by its participants. How liturgical ministers behave physically in the assembly is something all must endure. Ministers must not pose or seem pompous; neither should they be careless or seem to be self-conscious, flippant, or condescending. They must be and seem to be completely attuned to the nature of the event and the assembly celebrating it. A sense of natural physical grace in deportment, a sense of simple dignity, a certain self-discipline with regard to personal idiosyncrasies translate into a general impression by the assembly of its being respected and competently served by its liturgical ministers. The minister at the liturgy, like a Zen master, should be as "uninteresting" as a glass of cold, clear, nourishing water.

Smells: places where numbers of people gather over long periods of time develop distinctive odors, and the olfactory sense is as much a human faculty of communication as any other. Altering the familiar odor of a place, such as filling rooms with evergreens at Christmas, is normally a powerful act of communication without words. It defines space and time to be different from the ordinary, and thus it alters perceptions and expectations, often profoundly. Manufacturers of canned or bottled aromas know this fact very well and make their living off it. The liturgy knows the same fact equally well, which is why it has for so long used incense and aromatic chrism, in addition to lilies and evergreens, to mark times, places, and persons important to the assembly.

Touches: the liturgy also has traditionally placed high priority on the human sense of touch. A touch of a human hand, an embrace, the bathing and anointing of bodies all speak volumes about the assembly's confidence in things and people and in the commerce by which human and divine reality is constructed. For with touching without words goes an immense and risky ambiguity—an ambiguity which allows escape from the tyranny of words and texts and safe expectations, howsoever briefly.

2. *As does any art form, the liturgy gives enlarged room for imagination, for investment in and appropriation of values, and for freedom.*

The difference between a liturgy which does this and one which does not is the difference between art and propaganda, between creation and exploitation. A liturgy put together to foster some particular piety, devotion, or ideology is in violation of this principle.

3. *Liturgy is canonical.*

This means that the liturgy is an art constrained by rule, which is what *kanon* means in the original Greek. Every liturgical system in existence, Christian or not, is based on this principle simply because so highly complex a social art as liturgy must maintain a defined order of regular expectations lest it fail to be a participated event, one done by a host of different people for common purpose. One who would put Christian liturgy together must therefore be mindful of what the basic canons or rules are within the particular worship tradition of the assembly which will do such a liturgy. Traditional Christianity has maintained four such basic canons: 1) the canon of scripture, including both Old and New Testaments; 2) the canon of baptismal faith, the several Trinitarian creeds; 3) the canon of eucharistic faith, the eucharistic prayer or prayers of the Church's tradition; 4) the canon laws which have traditionally regulated the assembly's life both in the liturgy (e.g., the rubrics) and outside it (e.g., "canon law" in one form or another). To ignore these canons or rules runs the highest risk of leading the assembly into idiosyncratic dead ends, no matter how appealing these may appear to be at the moment.

4. *Liturgy is not adapted to culture, but culture to the liturgy.*

This reverses what one usually hears, namely, that the liturgy must be, and for the most part always has been, adapted to the culture in which it exists. Were this true, however, then the death of a culture either should result in the death of its liturgy (something not historically verifiable) or should indicate that the surviving liturgy never was wholly adapted to the deceased culture. More theologically, it is difficult to see how a Christian liturgy could remain faithful to the Gospel of Jesus Christ while allowing itself to become perfectly adapted to a culture hostile to that Gospel. In such a case, the liturgy would be supine before that which the assembly of faith is obliged to undercut, overturn, and reverse.

The culturalization process in the liturgy must therefore be different from this. There can be no doubt that the liturgy does indeed make use of forms and symbols it finds in culture. Pagan elements exist in the blessing of the font and the new fire ceremonies of Easter; the feast of Christmas was partly influenced by the Roman cult of the Unconquered Sun at the winter solstice. Yet neither Gospel nor Church nor liturgy became adaptively identified with any of the cultural elements. The assembly absorbed them as it renovated them to bespeak not their original pagan messages but the message of Jesus Christ. In this sense, the liturgy filtered, changed, preserved, and adapted cultural elements to itself, to the point that the only place one may still sense some elements of the vanished cult, say, of the Unconquered Sun, is in the Christian feast of Christmas.

The moral of this seems to be that the liturgical assembly is normally always in the business of absorbing cultural elements into itself in a rich diversity of ways and over long periods of time. The liturgy is not an artificial or abstract construct like Esperanto or computer language. It is more a lump of clay dug from the earth, shaped by people's hands, bearing their fingerprints, and sparked by divine genius in Christ if the people remain faithful in him. The liturgy thus survives cultures even as it adapts them to itself. The process can perhaps be monitored and remarked upon, but it probably cannot be forced or retarded for very long.

5. *Liturgy has more in common with an act of declamatory rhetoric than with scientific analysis or a classroom lecture.*

Liturgy is not a speech, but of the three sorts of speech mentioned it has more in common with the first than with the other two. This means that the liturgy declaims and proclaims something rather than it analyzes or teaches something. For this reason one should be serious, affirm forthrightly, avoid looseness and the commonplace, not annoy or polarize the assembly, and act with a gracious simplicity because humbug and mystification are foreign both to Christianity and its worship.

6. *In liturgy as in poetry, rhetoric, and music, meaning is as often communicated by rhythm and scale as by words alone.*

Liturgy is a ritual language, embracing far more than words and texts alone. One who would put a liturgy together cannot stop merely by getting straight the things to be said. Things to be done must also be considered, where they are to be done, and how they are to be done. Scurrying around the sanctuary in confusion suggests lack of clear purpose which even the most sensitive acts of presidency cannot smooth over. But stiff and rigid behavior is just as bad, suggesting that what one is watching is little more than a drill being done by rote. The constrained art of the liturgical "composer" requires higher degrees of forethought and creativity than this.

7. *Choose a liturgical style and hold to it.*

A liturgy of particular idiom such as the Roman, like a particular language, possesses its own logic and genius. This is ill served by throwing into it elements of alien idioms such as the Byzantine, rather as pretentious writers stuff their prose with foreign phrases. Syncretizing a liturgy with alien elements weakens its own logic and genius, making it more like a liturgical museum than a living act of worship. The best thing is to do the given assembly's liturgy straight.

8. *All possible liturgical options do not have to be implemented all at once.*

A Christian liturgical system like the Roman, which has enjoyed many centuries of development, contains a vast repertoire of texts, music, and ceremonies. In practice, this repertoire is much too vast to be used in its entirety by any one assembly. To bring as much of it as possible into use over the course of a year is something to which generations of liturgical experts have devoted perhaps more industry than pastoral good sense. This process was enhanced during the medieval period in the west, when the liturgy became an affair increasingly in the hands of clerical liturgical experts whose need for variety corresponded to the high quantity of liturgy they performed while the laity watched. The modern Roman Liturgy thus finds itself to be a rite of enormous variability, especially in its liturgies of the eucharist and the hours.

While all traditional Christian liturgical systems observe a certain variability, particularly in those parts proper to president, deacon, readers, and singers, all of them except the Roman keep the variability of the people's parts to a minimum. This enables the people to participate easily and by memory, especially in the eucharist of Sundays and feasts, when the full participation of the whole assembly is most crucial. For this reason, perhaps, other Christian liturgical systems have not suffered the cleavage between clerical and lay pieties, between liturgy and devotionalism, that was typical in the Roman system prior to the Second Vatican Council.

The notion on the part of many well-meaning people since the Council that this cleavage will be overcome by inducing the laity to take full part in the high variability which marked the clericalized medieval and counter-Reformation Roman Liturgy is a mistaken one. It mistakes an abnormality for the norm, for liturgy is not a clerical but a popular affair. It assumes that high variability is an aid to participation rather than an inhibition of it. It must then swamp the assembly with printed orders of service, printed collections of music all must sing, printed rubrical changes, practice sessions which distract and weary, and constant commentaries for the confused on how the event is going. All this confounds people, reduces many to passivity, and drives them away.

Good liturgy does none of this. It simplifies to the point that participation by the non-expert is facilitated without recourse to printed sheets, books, and practice sessions. Its variable parts are the responsibility of competent ministers; its invariable parts are the responsibility of everyone else, and the music for these parts must keep this in mind. Those responsible for putting liturgy together must realize that their task is one of keeping the high variability of the Roman Liturgy within acceptable limits for the vast majority of the assembly who are not, do not wish to be, and do not need to be liturgical experts. Responsible people will choose among the array of options contained in the reformed liturgical books so as to construct a basic public service which best serves the needs and abilities of the local assembly in context of its communion with the larger assembly of the Church universal and its traditions. This must be a work of high and creative responsibility. It must never be overwhelmed by fads, personal idiosyncrasies, or lack of authentic pastoral insight. It must be prosecuted by people who have the courage to obey the rubrics and the strength to resist being overwhelmed by them.

Some Matters of Form

Stoles

In the Roman Rite stoles are worn only by bishops, presbyters, and deacons. The latter wear them over the left shoulder. Other ministers never wear stoles, even over the right shoulder.

Concelebrations

The present usage of "verbal co-consecration" in the Roman Rite is, if not an abuse, an anomaly. Restored by the Second Vatican Council in order to "manifest the unity of the priesthood" rather than, as one might have hoped, the unity of the Church, its theory is flawed, its form verbally obsessive, its practice clericalizing, its use too frequent, and its numbers of concelebrants often gratuitously large.
Many clergy seem to feel that they cannot participate in the eucharist unless they verbally consecrate the sacrament, even if they must do so in suits from the pews. What such clergy do is analagous to a married couple refusing to take part in any eucharist not a nuptial mass. Such people forget that their ordination or marriage does not nullify their baptism, which they share at all times with the rest of the liturgical assembly.

The fact is that concelebration is a gesture of ministerial respect for the assembly, especially as the assembly observes events of special significance in its life, e.g., great feasts, visits of its bishop, ordination days, and the like. It should never be done merely as a convenience for supernumerary clergy without respect for the day or the size of the assembly. Nor should concelebrants usurp the functions of other liturgical ministers such as acolytes, readers, cantors, and deacons. All they rightly do is share discreetly the presidential role in the liturgy, supporting the one who presides without obscuring his function.

Incense

Incense is almost invariably used in world religions to enhance special times and places by sight and smell. In Christian eucharistic usage, it is effectively used at the beginning of the Service of the Word (during the entry) and at the beginning of the eucharistic banquet (at the preparation). Different types of incense might enhance various levels of solemnity throughout the year. It might well be omitted on penitential days and occasions, keeping in mind that Sunday is always festal, even during Advent and Lent. There seems to be no good reason to lavish attention on how a given liturgical event is to engage all the human senses except the olfactory. This sense, it has been pointed out, is perhaps the most subtly influential of them all; it continues to function even during sleep.

Jewelry

The wearing of jewelry by liturgical ministers is sev-
erly restricted in Roman canon law to bishops and
few others. The ascetical reasons for this should be
fairly obvious. So should the liturgical reasons, yet
this seems not to be the case. Austerity in altar ap-
pointments and vestments is made a mockery when
the liturgical minister displays personal jewelry of
apparent expense on hand, wrist, and chest. If the
minister's personal identity needs such supports,
they should be worn apart from the liturgy. In the
liturgy they should be taken off. This includes wrist
watches, especially the complex electronic kind,
which become distractingly visible at crucial
moments, such as during elevations, hand layings,
and blessings.

Devotion

Unhappily, liturgy and devotion have for centuries
developed in some divergence from each other in the
Roman Rite. As the liturgy became increasingly the
preserve of ecclesiastics, who codified it by law, it
began to lose touch with the people, who reacted by
developing devotional surrogates which largely escaped the strictures of liturgical law. Intensity of
emotion, fervor of prayer, and affectivity gradually
migrated into the devotional area as the liturgy itself
was divested of these same characteristics. Devotion
and liturgy came dangerously close to being antithet-
ical, even when the two were artificially wed, as
in the vernacular recitation of the Rosary or novena
during the parish mass, which was silent and in Latin.

This situation has changed noticeably since the Second Vatican Council introduced vernacular languages into the liturgy. The rich, if often excessive, devotional forms of preconciliar days were greatly diminished without, as it seems, transferring much of their intensity of emotion, fervor of prayer, and warm affectivity to the reformed liturgy. One may suspect that one reason for this is that the forms "devotionalism" had evolved were so essentially private in nature that their content was not much more transferrable to public liturgy than the devotional forms themselves.

Yet the liturgy of Christian churches has traditionally been home for intensity of emotion, fervent prayer, and warm affectivity—as one can still see in many Eastern Churches, which never suffered a separation between liturgy and affective devotion as the Roman Churches did. Restoration of these important characteristics in the Roman Liturgy is perhaps already under way; it is something that surely ought not to be resisted. But it will not be accomplished by inserting earlier devotional forms into the liturgy. It will be accomplished only by allowing those affective, prayerful, and emotion-laden elements already in the liturgy to recover from the atrophy they have suffered from during centuries of neglect. Such elements are those of deep reverence, rhythm, kisses of persons and things, gestures of courtesy, and the use of things which, when left to speak for themselves, are strong signs—water, oil, bread, wine, incense, color, movement, music, and gesture. Minimalism in these matters is not austerity; it is a bankruptcy which bespeaks nothing more than a lack of confidence in creation and the Gospel; a pious temerity at odds with the strong incarnationalism traditional Christian liturgy simply presupposes and cannot function without. The route to be taken is from "devotionalism" as an extraliturgical phenomenon to devotion restored in the liturgy's very heart.

Money

This means cash, which is one of the strongest symbols in an industrial and consumer oriented culture. Earlier societies exchanged largely in kind; modern western society exchanges regularly in paper or metal symbols whose significance is manifold and richly ambiguous. There is no tradition in the Roman Liturgy for how to handle cash as there is for handling gifts-in-kind. The collection of cash in the liturgy has thus come to be a utilitarian and secular interlude in the service, and its ritual significance in connection with the presentation of the gifts-in-kind accidental and obscure. Yet cash offering probably is more vigorously symbolic of a modern assembly's gift of itself than even the eucharistic gifts of bread and wine. This suggests that including the assembly's gifts of cash along with its gifts-in-kind ought to be standard procedure.

Announcements

There seems to be no perfect place to make announcements in the liturgy, and making them at the beginning of the homily, since it breaks gospel and homily apart, is perhaps the least perfect of all. The sixth-century papal mass put announcements at the beginning of communion, when there was some delay while the considerable numbers of ministers were busy preparing the plates of broken breads and the wine cups for the people. Another place might be just prior to the final blessing and dismissal. There seems to be no good reason why announcements should be kept out of the liturgy altogether and relegated to the bulletin, if there is one. Notification of events which are important to the assembly is part of its public business. But announcements should not disrupt the rhythmic flow of the service, and they should be kept to a minimum rather than be allowed to swell into an extended, rambling monologue by the president or others.

The Sign of Peace

The sign of peace was originally a full kiss on the lips, men with men, women with women. The kiss was perhaps the liturgy's most intimate gesture next to baptismal washing and anointing, so intimate indeed that the early church writers emphasize the need for it to be kept "pure", but kept nonetheless. We today kiss everyone and on all occasions except the liturgy, where, typically, we shake hands. The practice of shaking hands does not trigger as many symbolic resonances as the "pure" liturgical kiss does. The latter, unlike the former, presupposes people who are serious about their faith, indeed so serious as to be able to overcome cultural prohibitions against public intimacy. Whatever form the sign of peace takes in a given assembly—a kiss, an embrace, or a handshake—there is no reason why the liturgical ministers must transmit it to everyone in the church. Christ's peace is abroad among the faithful assembly itself. It is not mediated to all exclusively through the liturgical minister or the clergy.

Children

Membership in the faithful assembly knows no criteria of age, weight, education, or intelligence quotient—only those of faithful initiation into Christ in his Church. The criteria of faith for sacramental initiation are clear, rigorous, and just; the only criterion of faith after initiation is the living of a life faithful in Christ in his Church. Infants and children may do this in their own way just as well, if not better, than many adults. Be this as it may, the question is not one of the quality or extent of such living but of the rights, acquired through baptism and anointing, to live such a life. Living such a life implies and requires free access at all times to the sacraments of the liturgical assembly. Initiated infants and children may not be adolescents or adults, but they remain fully enfranchised members of the assembly by their sacramental initiation into it, and thus they should be treated as Christians possessing all the rights they are capable of exercising both actively and passively. They have, for example, a right to the assembly's liturgy; they, like other Christians, have no right to anything other than that. The Sunday liturgy is theirs no less than it is their pastor's or their parents'. And while they will need time and much special help in their growth into full and active participation in that Sunday liturgy, they must neither be nor appear to be disenfranchised of it. Their regular, if not always frequent, attendance at it is therefore not ideal but normal. If it bores them, it probably bores everyone else as well, and for the same reasons. This counsels that children may well be early and forceful witnesses to liturgical atrophy in their assembly, and that their witness should be taken seriously by all. Children learn much by vigorous ritual engagement, as Eric Erikson has pointed out. They learn perhaps even more by observing what ritual and liturgy do or do not do to adults, especially their parents, and to their peers and siblings. In view of this, children should never regularly be relegated to activities apart from the assembly's liturgy, and special liturgies for children should not so over-stimulate them on their own level as to make it hard for them to attend regular Sunday worship, or retard them liturgically on a childish level.

Hands

Next to the human face, hands are perhaps the most expressive parts of the human body. Their choreography runs the gamut of all human attitudes and emotions, as one can see in iconography and in classical ballet. In the liturgy one sees hands spread for prayer, folded in devotion, gracefully extended in invitation, and tracing signs of indication and blessing. When not in use they are best made invisible by leaving them at the sides, putting them beneath the chasuble, placing them at rest on a surface, or letting one hold the other in a relaxed manner at waist height. They should never drum or fidget with impatience, never go stiff with fright or tension, never go limp, or attempt to say more than hands can.

Postures

The human body, in its occupation of space, communicates much without words. The physical deportment of liturgical ministers is therefore of great importance: it should be relaxed and natural without suggesting informality, gracefully formal without being stiff or rigid. The problem with many liturgical ministers is not that their bodies say too little but that they say too much and say it badly. In processions ministers "march" in clots as though clinging to each other for comfort or support rather than spacing themselves well so that their movement takes on a modest significance. A procession is a parade, not a bus queue. Liturgical body language is an art of great understatement, and as such requires physical discipline. The marks of the chisel should never show.

Processions

There are in the Roman and most other eucharistic liturgies three processions which developed in response to the greater space needed by growing assembies after the fourth century. They are the entry procession; the procession with the eucharistic gifts of bread, water and wine; and the communion procession. The first two, since they usually involve fewer persons, require a degree of formality the last, which usually involves larger numbers, cannot hope to attain and does not need. All three are accompanied by singing, either psalm with antiphon or hymns. The entry, which is often protracted by ceremonial such as solemn veneration of the altar and the Gloria at its end, may be musically expanded by a sung litany as well, something which keeps up its rhythmic power at the liturgy's beginning when, during penitential seasons, the Gloria is omitted. Processions with litanies have traditionally been popular in the major Christian churches at times of penitence and special supplication. Their liturgical impact encourages popular participation due to their combination of movement and music into one strong rhythmic pattern.

Altar

The holy table is the physical focal point of every eucharistic place. It must never be overpowered by decorative architecture or suspended crosses; never compromised by the proximity of other major objects such as chair, tabernacle, or baptismal font; never trivialized by minor objects such as bookstands, microphones, cruets, flower vases, devotional aids and such like being left on it. Roman tradition, despite lapses here and there, has always regarded the holy table as the main architectural symbol of Christ's abiding presence among his people, recalling to them constantly their fundamental nature as a table fellowship in him. The table in this sense is a "blessed sacrament" in its own way and should be treated with the same degree of reverence accorded the sacrament of Christ's body and blood. That the integrity of both these sacred symbols of his abiding presence in the Church be maintained is the reason why the reformed liturgy reasserted the Roman tradition of reserving the eucharistic species in a place other than on the eucharistic place's holy table. Altar ornaments such as candlesticks, reliquaries, flower vases, crosses, and the like must be scaled to the table and are best removed when the table is not in use. The table itself should be free-standing, accessible from all sides, more square than long in shape, and itself scaled to the space it occupies. It should have a strong and elemental simplicity to it and possess a certain mass which remains visually constant from whatever angle it is viewed. The space around it should be flat and adequate to accomodate numbers of people and without complicated risers which endanger access and render the space fussy. The holy table is not an idol but a sacramental symbol of the presence of the Unseen. It is consecrated by water and oil similar to the way a Christian is consecrated in baptism.

Some Common Mistakes

Gratuitous concelebrations of the eucharist

Concelebrations are added to emphasize the unity of the Church especially on days of particular significance to the liturgical assembly. The actual number of concelebrants is determined by the size of the assembly and space available in the altar area. Phalanxes of concelebrants whose numbers overflow the sanctuary into the nave of the church constitute a violation of proportion and scale appropriate to the eucharistic event, running the risk of warping the assembly's perception of what it is and does. Concelebration is not an opportunity for presbyters to get in "their mass". It is not a clerical convenience, but an event to be used with appropriate discretion and in due scale so as to heighten the assembly's festive expression of its fundamental nature as the table fellowship with God in Christ.

Proliferation of ministers for reasons other than need

Liturgical ministry is not primarily an honor but a function of service in and to the Church assembled for divine worship. Loading sanctuaries with special ministers for ideological reasons, or to confer status and honor on special groups in the assembly, violates this fact and often has the effect of suggesting that the highest degree of Christian enfranchisement is to be found in clerical or quasiclerical status. The general principle is that ministers proliferate according to liturgical need, the need being determined by the assembly rather than by ideology. The assembly may indeed need a number of ministers beyond functional requirements at special times such as solemnities. In such a case, the need is real and should be met, but this is the exception rather than the rule, an abnormality rather than the norm. On such occasions in particular, it must be remembered that the fundamental principle is that every participant does those things, and only those things, appropriate to his or her liturgical role, ordained and unordained or special ministers included. Such special ministers do not take precedence over ordained ministers at liturgical events, but assist them as liturgical necessity dictates, in particular at communion time.

Disorderly practices at communion time

One such practice is that of having everyone help themselves to communion, as though the holy banquet were a buffet or a salad bar. The sacraments are ministries; they are served in assembly by its servants, who in doing so engage the entire assembly in a central requirement of the Gospel, that of being corporate servant in him who came not to be served but to serve. The transaction of ministerially serving the holy people of God is iconic of Jesus' own service at the Supper and to the world. It should not be omitted in favor of some egalitarian ideology. Servants presume the served.

Another such practice is that of snatching the host. The host is placed in the palm of the right hand, which is supported by the left hand beneath it. It is then raised to the mouth and reverently consumed. The hands should be carried in this manner as one approaches the one giving the host as an indication that the communicant wishes to receive in the hand, thus reducing the chance of misunderstanding and distracting mix-ups.

A final practice is that of grabbing the cup. Passing the cup back and forth between the minister and many communicants often results in spillage, and may even cause the cup to be dropped. One can reduce the probability of this sort of disedifying gaffe if the cup is held at its narrowest part by the minister as the communicant tips it to the lips by lifting the base. One should drink from the common cup. But if one has insurmountable scruples about doing this, one might hold the host up over one's palm to signal the minister that one will dip it slightly in the wine before consuming it. Individual cups, which are used in some Protestant Churches, represent an individualistic piety which is unliturgical and unknown in traditional Roman usage.

Breaking the bread at the words of institution

The president of the assembly is not a mimic whose task is to reproduce the Last Supper. He is a servant who serves the assembly in its celebration of the eucharist by proclaiming in its midst the motives for which it gives thanks. That on the night before he died, Jesus took bread, said the blessing, broke and gave it to his friends is a central motive for the assembly's giving thanks to God, but, as the eucharistic prayer itself makes clear, it is not the only one. The eucharist is not a mnemonic tableau of an historical event. It is a sweeping thanksgiving for the whole of the Father's benevolence toward the world and his people in Christ and the Holy Spirit. It does no more than what Jesus did in all the meals he took with those he loved. What he did at those meals quite escaped the bounds of any one meal on any one occasion. What he did was to make human beings free and forgiven table partners with God. Mimicking the details of what Jesus did at only one of those meals thus historicizes a mystery which transcends time and place, saying in the process far too little rather than too much. Christian liturgy is not an historical pageant. Presidents who cannot be convinced of this should not preside.

Confusing or ignoring the liturgical role of the deacon

The role of the deacon is now written clearly into the rubrics of the reformed Roman Liturgy on the supposition that this minister is a permanent fixture of Catholic ministry both inside and outside the liturgy. Unlike supernumerary ministers such as concelebrants or extra servers, the deacon is not added to the liturgy as an occasional enhancement but is presumed to be regularly present and functioning at all liturgical events. He is the assembly's prime minister: *Inter ministros primum locum obtinet diaconus (General Instruction on the Roman Missal*, para. 61). His ministry, whether in or out of the liturgy, is to the whole assembly in coordination with the ministries of bishop and presbyter. All the lesser ministries flow from and assist his ministry, discovering themselves in his as their source, paradigm, and coordinator. He should therefore be able to perform all of them at least as well as anyone else, which implies that he is server of servers, cantor of cantors, reader of readers. He is butler in God's house, *major domo* of its banquet, master of its ceremonies. Among other things, he does the following by right and duty:

Cares for and prepares the sacred vessels and the altar.

Oversees and directs all ceremonies and lesser ministries.

Leads litanies.

Reads the gospel and sometimes preaches.

Assists at the great elevation at the end of the eucharistic prayer.

Assists at the people's communion with the cup, from which he drinks last of all.

Gives directions for the assembly ("Let us kneel: Let us arise", "The Mass is ended. Go in peace", "Let us offer each other the sign of peace"), and makes other short announcements as necessary.*

Accompanies and assists the president as needed throughout the liturgy.

---

* Given this function, which is natural to his ministry, there seems no compelling reason why the deacon should not also announce "Let us proclaim the mystery of faith."

In the absence of lesser ministers, performs their duties as necessary.

Given the service (*diakonia*) emphasis of his office and ministry, the deacon (*diakonos*) is the most pronouncedly Christic of the three major ministries. This implies that it is not the bishop or presbyter who are liturgically "another Christ" (*alter Christus*), but the deacon.

Using secular greetings in the liturgy

The reason for which some presidents choose to greet the assembly with "Good morning, everybody" instead of "The Lord be with you" is difficult to fathom. It cannot be that the former is more appropriate to the assembly's purpose than the latter. Nor can it be that the first is theologically more sophisticated than the second. And since one would prefer not to entertain the possibility that the secular greeting is a mark of clerical condescension to the simple and untutored laity, the only alternative is to attribute the secular greeting's use to presidential thoughtlessness of a fairly low order.

Clericalizing the sign of peace

The practice of ministers, sometimes including the president, taking the sign of peace into the congregation not only delays the liturgy needlessly but suggests that the peace of Christ is mediated in the Church by its clergy. Neither scripture nor the liturgy itself supports such a view. In the Roman Liturgy the sign of peace, at least since the time of Gregory the

Great (+604), has been associated with the communal recitation of the reconciling Lord's Prayer. In most other Christian liturgical traditions it has been associated with the communal recitation of the reconciling Prayers of the Faithful, which conclude the service of the Word and begin the eucharistic preparation rite. In both cases, it is the common prayer of the whole assembly which prepares for exchange of the sign of peace. This suggests that the most appropriate procedure is for ministers and people to exchange the sign of peace among themselves where they stand and with their nearest neighbors. This is particularly appropriate at liturgies of some size and formality.

Changing texts well known to the assembly

Liturgical and biblical texts belong to the assembly. They do not belong to those who read them nor are they their playthings. The liturgical minister who cannot, for whatever reason, read the assembly's biblical and liturgical texts as they stand in the assembly's approved books should disqualify himself or herself from the assembly's liturgical ministry. Otherwise, the minister runs a high risk of polarizing the assembly by focussing attention upon the minister's own personal views about what he or she thinks is best for the assembly to hear. Such matters should be threshed out in forums other than that of the assembly's liturgical worship. These other forums exist in abundance.

General intercessions which are inaudible or polarize the assembly

In small, less formal liturgies it is sometimes well to have various members of the assembly offer informal extempore prayers of intercession. In larger liturgies, however, this practice is often counterproductive since the intercessions often cannot be heard by all. In such situations the intercessions should be done by deacon or cantor so that all may hear and respond, although nothing hinders members of the assembly from requesting that specific intentions be included. In either situation one should remember that general intercessions are normally just that, namely, general—for Church, the world, the society, peace, and categories of special need, such as the ill, bereaved, travellers, the suffering, etc. As a rule, general intercessions do not become personal or name names: these names might be read out before the general intercessions begin. The general intercessions must be expressed in such a manner that they do not alienate or "excommunicate" persons or groups in the assembly. Christians at worship do not pray against some things or persons but, like Christ, they always pray for all persons and things, leaving him who sees into hearts and motives to be their judge. The general intercessions summon the Church in unity to pray. They are not sermonettes meant to rend the assembly so that prayer is impossible for all but the ideologically pure, and the sacrament of unity unachievable.

Ignoring the liturgical year

Liturgical ministers sometimes forget what retailers know well and wholesalers live from, namely, that times and seasons are both artifacts and shapers of the human psyche. Seasonal change changes people individually and in groups; they buy, think, and live differently. Christian liturgy, with its profound sacramentalism, has traditionally exploited this fact to the fullest. It is thus difficult to understand why some ministers think it a peculiar Christian relevance to compromise or wipe out liturgical times and seasons in favor of "theme masses" which concentrate on doctrinal or ideological exploitation of current issues. This reveals the didactic fallacy at work in the assembly; it reduces the eucharist to an occasion for doing something else, the Gospel to a teacher's manual, the assembly to the passivity of the taught, the Church to a socio-educational movement, and the ministry to a group of ideologues.

Minimalism and pontificalism

Minimalism and pontificalism represent the two unacceptable extremes in degree of liturgical usage. The first sins by symbolic and ceremonial defect, the second by symbolic and ceremonial excess. Both are constant whether the service is small and intimate or large and formal. Pontificalism is always swollen, overblown, and fussy; minimalism is always shrunken, desiccated, and perfunctory. Pontificalism's services are always heavy, placing too much emphasis on tertiary elements to the point of obscuring the primary. Minimalism's services are always insubstantial, placing not enough emphasis on anything. It is pontificalism which breeds the rumor that solemnity is synonymous with complexity, heavy-handedness, and boredom in the assembly;

minimalism which breeds the rumor that being solemn about solemn things is a vice. Yet there is nothing more solemn and simple, grave and limpidly clear, than an extended act of Zen communal meditation; a Byzantine liturgy in Hagia Sophia which, witnessed by the astonished ambassadors of Vladimir of Kiev, converted Russia to Christianity; an episcopal liturgy in the city of Rome which fired the imagination of the barbaric peoples of Europe. A liturgy which descends into either minimalism or pontificalism is the result of an assembly's and its ministers' having lost the evangelical discipline which the gospels, the apostolic writers, and the tradition both inculcate and presuppose.

An Approach to Liturgical Style

Until now this book has been concerned with what is correct or acceptable in liturgical usage. Now it must speak of style in its broadest meaning, style in E.B. White's sense of what is distinguished and distinguishing. Here one leaves solid ground. For who can say with certainty why one liturgy done quite without music and with little ceremonial elaboration seems heavy, complex, and dull, while another of greater length and more solemn scale seems light, simple, and engaging—both liturgies being correct in their own ways?

Style involves taste, and taste is not innate. It must be learned through social intercourse. The maxim that taste is not arguable does not mean that matters of taste are too subjective to be debated profitably. It means that taste is so radically a public matter that its elements fall beyond the exclusive competency of private feelings. If, for example, one is obtuse enough not to sense the inappropriateness of slapping the British monarch on the back or of condescending to the poor, then one has become so numb to the human condition as to be incapable of discoursing profitably about taste. *De gustibus non disputandum imbecilibus*. Taste is an intrinsically social matter without which style is impossible, taste being to style what grammar is to poetry.

But liturgical style is not simply an esthetic matter, despite the fact that esthetics are inevitably involved. For the liturgy is not the Church's esthetic *latreia* but its *logike latreia*, its reasonable or spiritual, as opposed to carnal, service—a service not of fleshly feeling but of *logos*, of rigorous intellectual and spiritual meaning.

The *logos*-meaning of the Church's peculiar *latreia* is to be found only in a total view of God, humanity, and the world in Jesus Christ. This view begins with an orthodox grasp of God as a communion of Persons who throw open their mutual communion to others. Thus humankind was created in the image of One who would camp in its midst, realizing therein a total, actual, and abiding communion between Creator and creature on the most concrete level. The *logos*-meaning the Church's peculiar *latreia* of liturgical service thus requires a holistic cosmology of redemption.

Creation's history is in this view a progressive revelation of the Creator's self-giving for humankind. Creation is one great and loving sacrificial liturgy in which the presider solicits the free concelebration of our race in communion with him for the life of the world. In this, the initiative is wholly his rather than ours. That we are able to love him at all means quite simply that he has loved us first. The communion of divine Persons projects itself into space and time first by creative act, an act by which all things come to be and remain in being.

Our discovery of communality among creatures is a small glimpse into the Source of all things. That Source we discover to be a communion of Persons communicating Its Self in space and time. The world we discover to be not merely a random aggregation of separate and abutting existences but an articulated whole, an interdependent "ecology" of existences, all of which commune really if differently in their common Source, a triune God. We perceive this truly if only dimly in the relationship among creatures of male, female, and offspring; among humans of lover, beloved, and love's offspring—of mother, father, child.

The incarnation in space and time of One who proceeds eternally from the Father is both foundation stone and rooftree of creation's communion in its Source. The very paradox of an enfleshed *Logos* is archetype of our race's return from alienation into that same communion. That existence of the *Logos* in the flesh results from a divine initiative assented to freely by her who is the splendid representative of us all. In her the Unmade submits to the strictures of human generation, the Ungrowing to the discipline of human growth, the Unfailing to the risk of human frustration and failure. The enfleshed *Logos* thus takes his place as the mediator, priest, and president of creation's concelebration of its reunion with its Source. The sacrificial liturgy of God's love for us has reached its endless climax, for ". . . in Christ Jesus, we who used to be so far apart have been brought close by the blood of Christ. For he is the peace between us, and has made the two into one and broken down the barrier which used to keep us apart, actually destroying in his own person the hostility caused by the rules and decrees of the Law. This was to create one single new Man in himself out of us and, by restoring peace through the cross, to unite us in a single Body reconciling us with God . . . Through him, we have in one Spirit our way to come to the Father" (*Ephesians* 2:13-18). Jesus Christ is thus the primary sacrament not only of our encounter with, but of our communion in, God with all God's holy things and all God's holy people—dead, born, and yet unborn.

This means that the Church, the gathering, the assembly, the household of faith "where God lives, in the Spirit" (*Ephesians* 2:22), is the living corporate mode throughout the rest of time and space of Christ's personal enfleshment. It is the abiding presence of his own sacramentality, the free and open manifestation of his victory over dispersion, separation, and alienation among all God's creatures. It therefore stands in witness against egotistical individualism, being constituted by God in Christ "a chosen race, a royal priesthood, a holy nation, God's own people" (1 *Peter* 2:9). What it celebrates is the cosmic liturgy of the union of all in the unique Source of all. This liturgy is conjunctive, never disjunctive. It is grace witnessing against sin.

It is into this that baptism splices one, giving life in Christ's Body, a life of communion both in the triune God and in a humanity restored according to that same communality. This life is never merely individualistic and passive but always public and active, being deeply personal and in sustained relationship with others. Baptized life is ensemble life. To live it is to live deep in symbol, deep in meaning, deep in ritual, deep in style, deep in liturgical expression because to live socially is to live this way. It is to live free of all that would drag one down into the antitheses of life—egotism, obsession, fear, alienation, limit, meaninglessness, random facticity, death. Those who have come home do not live in such a way. Nor do they live in a self-serving ghetto whose main purpose is the bare survival of the social group. Both as individuals and as groups, Christians are aware that survival is had only by throwing life away. Perduring life lies not in the gift of social structures, nature, the psyche, physical processes, nor of this or that system. It lies only in the gift of life's Source, the deathless-because-uncreated ensemble of the Godhead itself. For one to choose anything less than this is to choose to die finally and without hope of survival. For a Christian, to live is to live at one with the world's Source by sense, mind, and spirit.

This is the *logos* of Christian faith-life which the liturgy simply presupposes. The liturgy in this perspective is nothing other than the ceremonial of *logos*, the ritual of the Word of life's meaning, the enacted style of the world's meaning. To the extent that the liturgy degenerates into little more than an enforcement of some systemic status quo, a living tableau for theological or social polemics, or an exercise in subjective egotism, the liturgy becomes nothing but the first symptom of apostasy from the whole Christian *logos* of meaning. Such a liturgy, furthermore, not only signals such an apostasy but helps cause and sustain it as well. For this reason, if for no other, liturgy is serious business: it can never be taken lightly, for its meaning, its *logos*, is life itself.

LITERARY ANALOGIES

There can be no doubt that the Christian *logos*-meaning sketched so far transcends every specific liturgical idiom as meaning transcends every specific literary style. As one can live Christian *logos* liturgically as Byzantine or Copt, Anglican or Roman, Armenian or Lutheran, so also one can engage human meaning—such as the meaning of filial love or of civic order—in a variety of cultural styles. One can also engage and express meaning in a variety of literary styles.

One may thus view liturgical endeavor as an increment to *logos* as style (whether cultural or literary) is incremental to human meaning. This means that a liturgical idiom or event is not *logos* any more than style is meaning, or education and social formation are a human being. Liturgy, style, education and social formation are increments to larger and more radical realities. But these larger and more radical realities, i.e., meaning and being human, become operational and intensified only in their incremental dimensions. An organism, for example, may be essentially human without educational or social increments, but such an organism rarely becomes operationally humane except by such incremental processes as education and social interaction with others of the same species. The potentialities inherent in the human organism are there to be actualized. The same may be said of meaning and its actualizing increment, style.

The poet Herrick could have disclosed essential meaning by stating the bare fact that he loved Julia without resorting to any stylistic increment. What Herrick did say, however, was this:

Whenas in silks my Julia goes,
Then, then, methinks, how sweetly flows
The liquefaction of her clothes.

The bare and essential meaning of his love for Julia is not only still there, but by the increment of style it has been powerfully actualized so as to operate also upon others. This is so, at least in part, because the oblique way the essential meaning is expressed is reverentially intriguing: it simultaneously exposes and shrouds the beloved. Herrick's devotion is carried in the simple image of a female figure moving in a rustling silken dress, the coolness and smoothness of which suggests Herrick's love to be elevated, formal, shot through with a reverent elegance so intense that his bodily senses are flooded with Julia. His lines are a sensuous icon which even the ears can hear in the sibilance of language. Not only has the increment of

style positively universalized Herrick's love by focussing intensely on the specific object of his love in a
compelling manner, but it has rendered that love
deathless for all those who have ever heard silk
move. The meaning of one human being's love for
another has been suffused with a quality which is as
permanent as it is impossible to put into the prose of
a position paper.

But even more than this happens. One steps away
from so superb an act of language irrevocably
changed in one's address to existence itself. One
realizes, for example, that the unknown Julia and her
lover have both long since returned to the septic elemental particles from which all things are made, and
one is stunned with the splendid pity of it all. One is
freed to associate the unassociable—perhaps the cool
green elegant love of these two with Thomas Wolfe's
lines, "Quick are the mouths of earth, and quick the
teeth that fed upon this loveliness." Stylish increment
intensifies meaning and injects it into the larger experience of the race, freeing imagination and overwhelming the emotions and senses along the way. A
human transaction has been consummated within
the *res publica* of our discourse and condition.

All writing communicates meaning, but writing that
has style communicates meaning through revelation.
In E. B. White's felicitous phrase, "It is the Self escap-
ing into the open". Every act of style represents the
writer seducing others into the meaning revealed,
not by enslavement but by liberation. Nor is style a
mere garnish to prose, something separate from

meaning. It is a quality one discovers as one really works at perceiving the meaning all things possess. The approach to it, White counsels, is by way of plainness, simplicity, orderliness, and sincerity.

All this is correspondingly true of Christian *logos* and liturgical style, but in greater degree of complexity. A liturgy is not a line of words written only by one author; a liturgy is not a text but a whole series of acts, words, gestures, sights, sounds, and smells in constant if not always perceptible evolution; a liturgy's authors are not individuals but whole generations of Christians. The style of a liturgical idiom such as the Roman is less like that of a poem written by one poet at a particular time than it is like the style of a whole language system in constant composition by all those who speak it over the span of generations.

Liturgical style is nonetheless to *logos* as literary style is to meaning. Christian *logos* is that larger and more radical reality which transcends any and all of its liturgical increments. Yet these liturgical increments render *logos* actual, operational, effective, and gripping in ways native to a given Christian group. Thus the triune God's will to commune with humanity beyond the Law, even to an outpouring into the strictures of time, space, and alienated human malevolence, can never be left as a prosaic statement of fact any more than Herrick's love for Julia could have been left by him at the level of a flat and factitious statement.

A Christian liturgy will bespeak its *logos* of meaning in a style that strains to embrace and articulate not just words but the whole of creation—in fire and water, dust and ashes, oil and perfume, bread and wine, soaring sounds and tender gestures; in times of joy and bereavement, at times crucial in nature's course as well as in the course of individuals and whole societies; in social categories, in poems of violence and hymns of peace, in silence as well as in noisy jubilation; with living plants and animals as well as with dead wood and lifeless stone; in movement and in stillness, laughter and tears, by speaking and listening and keeping quiet; by celibacy for some and sexual activity for others and chastity for all; in tombs and bath houses and dining rooms, wherever people meet to transact reality. Christian liturgy must do all this because the *logos* it increments under grace is just this all-encompassing. Its meaning fills all things, in time and beyond.

One steps away from a superb act of liturgy, in which one has communed palpably not only with one's own self or one's immediate neighbor but with the divine Persons immersed in the life of the world, changed in one's whole address to existence itself. When one remembers, for example, all the unknown people over the past five thousand years who have loved this same vast mystery and transmitted it to one in this place and time, one is moved by the splendid pity of it all. And one is freed to associate the unassociable—the deathless, uncreated, and timeless Creator of all with the simple human creatures of bread broken and wine poured out to rejoice mortal hearts.

In such a frame, Herrick's lines of love for Julia, Wolfe's lines on an omniverous springtime, Robert Frost's stopping by cold woods, Walt Whitman's delight in laughing flesh, take on vastly greater power. They are swept up into this transcendental *logos* of meaning when they enter the sensibility of faith. For when God becomes man then all these lines apply parabolically, and "Quick are the mouths of earth, and quick the teeth that fed upon this loveliness" throbs like an antiphon as we, whom he loved more than any man can love a woman, nail his laughing flesh to the cold wood of the cross.

Style raises meaning to revelation. Liturgy increments *logos* by revealing its style in a people's life in faith, allowing that people's corporate Self to escape into the open where it discovers creation coming always new from God, already evangelized by his living Word, and humankind restored to communion with him who is all in all by the self-giving of his incarnate *Logos*, Jesus Christ. Given this, that people's corporate Self, now free and in the open, cannot but imagine such a God in such a Christ forevermore walking the world's roads, dining with the poor, gazing at one from the eyes of a friend, speaking to a farmer through the success or failure of his crops, consoling parents who have lost a child by giving them his own self as food and drink. In these and in a million other tiny ways which form the fabric of existence for those who believe in him, the Source of all concelebrates what it is to be among those who share in divine *logos*. And that concelebration is the liturgy of a restored world in a given place and time, the world done as its Source and Redeemer would have the world done.

Every liturgical act is the assembly succumbing to *logos* revealed, to the freedom *logos* bears within it. Nor is liturgy mere garnish for the meat of *logos*, mere sauce by which a dull dish of gospel is made palatable. Liturgy is a quality faithful people discover in existence as they really work at grasping the *logos* with which God has impregnated all things. The beginner should therefore approach the liturgy warily, understanding it to be nothing less than one's social faith-self which is being approached. One should begin by turning resolutely away from all devices that are popularly believed to indicate something or someone as "liturgical"—mannerisms, tricks, adornments such as bizarre vestments, prayers in foreign accents, ornate and heavy ceremonial, wordy banners, and state trumpets. The approach to liturgy, as to literary style, is by way of plainness, simplicity, orderliness, and sincerity. Every fugue begins with one note, every poem with one word, every building with one stone.

For most this is laborious and slow. The minister's liturgical imagination often travels faster than do the abilities of most congregations to learn new liturgical patterns or unlearn old ones. God issues *logos*, not rubrics. It is useful to remember that Jesus in the days of his flesh submitted to the liturgical style of his people and his time. He changed no ceremony in Israel but observed them all, from Passover Seder to Sabbath requirement to temple sacrifice. How he transformed it all was not by ceremonial reform but by revealing himself as its *logos*, its meaning, and then by gathering it all into himself. "Today in your presence," he said, "is this text fulfilled". "This bread of affliction", he said, "is my body. This cup of blessing is my blood poured out for you". The temple's sacrifice walked abroad in him.

The primary stylistic task of the liturgist is thus not to tinker with ceremonies but to bespeak *logos* within the assembly as it enacts its spiritual sacrifice of praise and thanksgiving in Christ. A liturgist who merely tinkers with ceremonies is no more a liturgist than one who merely tinkers with language is a poet. Any approach to liturgical style requires work and patience. One must wait diligently upon God in prayer and contemplation. One must study. One must also wait diligently upon the assembly one serves and in which one lives. The following are some hints and cautions towards these ends.

1. *Place yourself in the background.*

One should engage in liturgy so that attention is called to *logos* rather than to one's own virtuosity. Liturgical mastery will eventually be revealed, but not at the expense of *logos*. The liturgical minister will begin by affecting nothing that calls untoward attention to himself or herself. One who is careful, informed, and sincere will not have to worry about the liturgy very much. The liturgical minister is not the poet but only the reciter of the poet's poem—the poet in this case being the Christian assembly past and present. As the minister develops competency in liturgical service, he or she will find it increasingly less difficult to commune with other communicants in Christian *logos* liturgically enacted. This is the purpose of all liturgical ministry as well as its greatest reward. Furthermore, developing liturgical competence disciplines the mind and heart of the minister; it is one way to go about praying, and the habit of praying both drains the mind and supplies it as well.

2. *Do things naturally.*

One must serve Christian *logos* in the assembly's liturgical worship in ways that come easily and naturally to one, using words and gestures which come readily to hand. But one can never be wholly confident that, because one acts in a manner that feels natural to one, the product will always be above reproach. For what seems natural may well be perceived by the assembly as either too little or too much, as idiosyncratic and distracting. It is easy to confuse personal style with individual self-indulgence. Ultimately it is the liturgical assembly which decides what is natural in its liturgical servants, and to this decision the minister must be both attentive and obedient. Liturgical service that passes this test will echo the good things in the particular liturgical tradition that bear being seen and heard again. Mastery of liturgical service, like mastery of language, begins with imitation and continues to imitate long after one is on one's own, for it is nearly impossible to avoid imitating what is admirable. This takes ministerial discipline and great humility.

3. *Know the assembly's liturgical tradition thoroughly.*

Each liturgical tradition has its own vocabulary and grammar. And while all the traditions share some central words and grammatical constructions in general, they remain specifically distinct. The same might be said, for example, of English and German languages: they share many common words and some constructions, but one who speaks only one cannot be understood by one who speaks only the other. To write English according to German grammar produces comic English, as Mark Twain demonstrated in his essay, "The Awful German Language".

Something similar can occur liturgically when a liturgist who is either ignorant or uncaring attempts to syncretize different liturgical idioms of very different styles. A Roman Catholic "Covenant Service" is as anomalous as a Methodist pontifical mass; each baffles the respective assembly's access to *logos* and, as such, represents some degree of pastoral irresponsibility on the part of each assembly's ministers. It is better by far to take one's liturgical tradition straight and deal with it responsibly, for it represents the way one's assembly has come to perceive and enact Christian *logos*, for better or worse.

4. *Do the liturgy with directness and vigor.*

A liturgical act filled with gratuitous flourishes such as changes of vestments, doffings of hats, minor processions, complicated service sheets, prolix prayers, and bombastic sermons is like a sentence filled with adjectives. Such things trivialize both literary meaning and Christian *logos* by qualifying too much. They may even obstruct access to *logos* altogether. The same may occur in the modern flight into informality, where the intricate details of seeming not to discern, discriminate, or take a position (things required by formality) devour substantive aspects of the rite, thereby shrouding *logos* in a fog of role confusion and shallow self-effacement techniques. This is not humility. It is time-consuming temerity of a low order, an elaborate mechanism for avoiding responsibility and accountability. It renders *logos* dubious by reducing its liturgical enactment to the level of a concelebrated uncertainty and the Church to an assembly without evangelical or missionary thrust—a sheepfold enclosing the unsure and the bemused. The *logos* of God's self-revelation in Christ is worth more than this.

One must remember that the outcome of any act of style, literary or liturgical, is that it allows the individual and corporate Self to escape into the open. A liturgy, like a good poem, frees. The poem frees one into the large and radical meanings of human existence. The liturgy frees a whole assembly into the large and radical *logos* of the divine communion with all that is in Christ Jesus. Both acts must therefore be done with a simple directness and vigor congruent with the purpose of each.

5. *Beware of particularizing the liturgy.*
A superb act of language, no matter who its speaker or what its immediate audience, does not long re-

main the singular possession of the particular group. This is so because such an act changes not only speaker and hearer but the whole context of meaning from which words proceed. A superb act of liturgy, similarly, can never be the sole possession of a single assembly or of any special group within an assembly. It is the whole Church which worships, and through it the whole of a restored world. For as Christian *logos* is communitarian, so is its liturgical agent and the style of that agent, the assembly. The liturgy of the assembly is always a local act but is never particularized as the sole possession of the local group. Because liturgy enacts the large and radical *logos* of the divine communion with all that is in Christ Jesus, it always escapes into the open of divine and human universality. A liturgy which fails to attain this dimension is little more than the assembly indulging itself. As such, it is in violation of Christian *logos*.

6. *Beware of liturgical fundamentalism.*

Fundamentalism of whatever sort is a mindless regression into fantasy undertaken out of an obsessive fear of risk and ambiguity. Fundamentalists produce not poetry but propaganda, not liturgy but self-serving bible study groups. The liturgy, on the other hand, like a language system, is shot through with the rich ambiguity of metaphor, symbol, sacrament, and it is always changing even when it appears not to be. No more than the liturgy can afford to be celebrated in nothing but third, thirteenth, or sixteenth century ceremonial forms can a modern poet afford to write in nothing but Chaucerian English. One must not confuse liturgical archaism, which is native to times of high religious significance, with liturgical fundamentalism, which is constant and obsessive.

7. *Do not over-ceremonialize.*

One whose taste for intricate or arcane ceremonial causes one to lose one's grip on *logos* is like a writer whose taste for orotund expression causes meaning to be obscured. Ceremony and literary style are important matters, but each is subordinated to ends that lie beyond themselves. For liturgical ceremony this end is the Christian *logos* enfleshed in an assembly's way of life in faith. For literary style this end is meaning shared.

8. *Do not affect a loose informality.*

The one thing Christians have been doing most for the past two thousand years is meeting for formal worship in common. For some churches this is about all they have ever done; for some modern churches this is about all totalitarian states permit them to do. The sheer quantity of formal Christian worship is therefore enormous. Much modern western liturgical worship, however, has a loose informality about it which seems to reflect a kind of euphoric optimism unwarranted by a steady hold on reality.

Breezy liturgical style is not characteristic of one who has attained liturgical mastery. It is usually the work of an egocentric who imagines that whatever occurs to him or her is generally interesting and that uninhibited liturgical expression of this will create enthusiasm and carry the day. It may also be a compensation mechanism of the guilt-ridden or unsure who cannot cope with the fact that some of God's ways are inscrutable and often illiberal according to human standards. Whatever the motive, the Spontaneous Me approach to liturgy produces little prayers, rambling homilies on current events, sappy hymns, and eucharists hardly distinguishable from the coffee and dougnut social that follows in the church hall. That the taste of all this is dubious or its discipline minimal is not the point. The point is that it is untrue. It warps Christian *logos* into a liturgical style which that *logos* does not support but condemns. For that *logos* is not about becoming well-adjusted in a world where, by human choice, death is at home. It is about breaking through such a world into another, where life that passes all understanding, and is available only at immense cost, is discovered to have been our birthright all along. This is the real world, that for which we were created and redeemed on a cross. Anything less is fantasy and fable.

This does not mean that liturgy must be glum. It means that the liturgy's joy lies on a level deeper than can be attained by mere good humor and gusty behavior in church. The liturgical joy native to Christian *logos* is steady and disciplined, a wisdom which takes reality whole and straight. No human paradox is alien to it, no mystery is avoided or resolved. It steadfastly ignores the merely current. It transcends ideology, strips away illusion, overturns status quo, and convinces of sin. "The *logos* of God is something alive and active. It cuts like a two-edged sword, but more finely. It slips through the place where soul separates from spirit as bone from marrow. It judges secret emotions and thoughts. No creature can hide from him; everything is uncovered and open to the eyes of the one to whom all must account for themselves" (*Hebrews* 4:12-13).

God's justice runs in the liturgy's veins as does his mercy. Both require the liturgy's participants to enter utterly naked as from a womb and to leave utterly naked as into a tomb. For one can bring nothing of this dying world into it, and it will give one nothing of this dying world to take out. The liturgy's supreme act of festivity takes the form of banqueting on the body and blood of the *logos* enfleshed, the body and blood of us all, and what it proclaims is his death until he comes, the death of us all, for we are a people graced even in our brokenness. In this great and mysterious liturgy we sink down to the deepest point from which all reality proceeds. A loose informality is inappropriate here.

9. *Do not explain too much.*

If a poet must explain the poem before it is recited, there is something wrong with the poem. If a liturgy must be explained before it is done, there is something wrong with the liturgy. In such cases it is probable that there is something wrong with the poet and the liturgist as well. This is not to say that preparation is never needed. It is only to say that lengthy explanations are always abnormal and should never occur as an immediate prelude to the act itself. The assembly needs sustained preparation and formation of various sorts—evangelical, homiletical, catechetical, and ascetical. It is when these are lacking that last-minute recourse is had on the part of slothful ministers to verbose explanations of what is about to happen. The risk this runs is that of turning the liturgy into a "learning experience", as it is called. In a culture such as ours the educational temptation is difficult to resist. But liturgy which is stylish and effective in incrementing *logos* leads not to the brink of clarity but to the edge of chaos. It deals not with the abolition of ambiguity but with the dark and hidden things of God. When it comes to liturgy, precision can be bought at too high a price, and some things cannot be said.

10. *Strive for simplicity.*

Simplicity is noble. It is not the same as barren brevity. Rhythm requires repetition and time. Solemnity, on the other hand, does not require slowness, ponderousness, or weight. Solemnity should skip rather than trundle, dance rather than lumber. Solemnity and simplicity are close to being the same thing, and each is native to a liturgy which is divine service.

11. *Do not get too relevant.*

This year's relevancies are often next year's embarrassments. One who does not appreciate this should meditate on the Nehru Jacket and Death of God movement. The liturgy frees one from such compulsions. It must not succumb to them.

12. *Learn to live with symbol.*

One who is convinced that symbol and reality are mutually exclusive should avoid the liturgy. Such a one should also avoid poetry, concerts and the theater, language, loving another person, and most other attempts at communicating with one's kind. Symbol is reality at its most intense degree of being expressed. One resorts to symbol when reality swamps all other forms of discourse. This happens regularly when one approaches God with others, as in the liturgy. Symbol is thus as native to liturgy as metaphor is to language. One learns to live with symbol and metaphor or gives up the ability to speak or to worship communally.

13. *Adapt culture to the liturgy rather than liturgy to culture.*

Adapting liturgy to culture invariably results in the liturgy's demise. Adapting culture to the liturgy is thus the only alternative, a far more demanding endeavor, but one worthy of *logos*. This is not to say that liturgy can exist apart from culture; only that liturgy must not chase after and lend support to cultural trends. People who do liturgy inevitably live in and are immersed in a culture, the more the better. Thus liturgy, the act of such people, can avoid culture no more than fish can avoid water. Yet the liturgy sustains a certain ascetical tension in relation to its cultural milieu for *logos'* sake. Liturgy sympathizes, so to speak, with its culture's plight, but it never seeks to give cheap or superficial fixes for its culture's wants. The liturgy's duty is to enflesh and serve *logos*, and true liturgy celebrates nothing but the active presence of Three in all. Let liturgy start sniffing the cultural air or start tracking its fads and bestsellers and it is as good as dead. It becomes like a gifted poet who throws it all up to write doggerel for television commercials. Liturgy either dies at the hands of the Trendy, or it slays them. Neither alternative is comfortable, but the last is what Christian *logos* ultimately requires.

Bibliography

Sources

The following are some recent official sources touching matters raised in this book. For exhaustive listings of such sources the reader is referred to the books of Seasoltz and Richstatter listed under Studies, below.

Bishop's Committee on the Liturgy, *Environment and Art in Catholic Worship*. NCCB, Washington 1978.

Congregation for Divine Worship, "On Dance in the Liturgy," *Notitiae* 11 (1975) 202-205.

Constitution on the Sacred Liturgy, *Sacrosanctum Concilium* (1963), in *The Documents of Vatican II*, ed. Walter M. Abbot. America Press, New York 1966 (cited hereafter as Abbot), 137-178.

Dogmatic Constitution on the Church, *Lumen Gentium* (1964), in Abbot, 14-96.

Instruction on the Worship of the Mystery of the Eucharist, *Inaestimabile Donum* (1980). "Instructio de quibusdam normis cultum Mysterii Eucharistici," *Notitiae* 16 (1980) 287-296.

The Mystery and Worship of the Holy Eucharist, *Dominicae Cenae* (1980), an encyclical letter of Pope

John Paul II, in Edward J. Kilmartin, *Church,*
Eucharist, and Priesthood: A Theological Commentary
on the Mystery and Worship of the Most Holy
Eucharist. Paulist Press, New York 1981, 69-100.

The New Order of Mass, *Institutio Generalis Missalis*
Romani (1969). *The New Order of Mass*, transl. by the
Monks of Mt. Angel Abbey. The Liturgical Press, Collegeville, Minnesota. 1969. This is also printed in the
front of *The Sacramentary: The Roman Missal*, revised
by decree of the Second Vatican Council and pub-
lished by authority of Pope Paul VI. ICEL-NCCB.
Catholic Book Publishing Co., New York 1974.

Studies

Adam, Adolf, *The Liturgical Year: Its History and Its*
Meaning after the Reform of the Liturgy, transl. Mat-
thew J. O'Connell. Pueblo Publishing Co., New
York 1981.

Baumstark, Anton, *Comparative Liturgy*, transl. F. L.
Cross. A. R. Mowbray, London 1958.

Bloomer, Kent C. and Charles W. Moore, *Body, Mem-*
ory, and Architecture. Yale University Press, New
Haven 1977.

Bouyer, Louis, *Liturgical Piety*. University of Notre
Dame Press, Notre Dame, Indiana 1954.

Burkhart, John E., *Worship. A Searching Examination of*
the Liturgical Experience. Westminster Press, Philadel-
phia 1982.

Dehne, Carl, "Roman Catholic Popular Devotions,"
Christians at Prayer, ed. John Gallen. University of
Notre Dame Press, Notre Dame, Indiana 1977. 83-99.

Erikson, Eric H., "Ontogeny of Ritualization in Man," in *Philosophical Transactions of the Royal Society of London*, Series B, No. 772, Vol. CCLI (1966) 337-350.

Fast, Julius, *Body Language*. M. Evans and Company, New York 1970.

Grainger, Roger, *The Language of the Rite*. Darton, Longman and Todd, London 1974.

Hall, Edward T., *The Hidden Dimension*. Doubleday Anchor Books, Garden City, New York 1966.

Holmer, Paul, "About Liturgy and Its Logic," *Worship* 50 (1976) 18-28.

Hovda, Robert W., *Dry Bones. Living Worship Guides to Good Liturgy*. The Liturgical Conference, Washington 1973.

Hovda, Robert W., *Strong, Loving and Wise: Presiding in Liturgy*. The Liturgical Conference, Washington 1976.

Huels, John M., "The Interpretation of Liturgical Law," *Worship* 55 (1981) 218-237.

Irwin, Kevin W., *Sunday Worship*. Pueblo Publishing Company, New York 1982.

Kavanagh, Aidan, "How Rite Develops: Some Laws Intrinsic to Liturgical Evolution," *Worship* 41 (1967) 334-347.

Kavanagh, Aidan, "The Role of Ritual in Personal Development," in *The Roots of Ritual*, William B.

Eerdmans Publishing Company, Grand Rapids, Michigan, 1973, 145-160.

Manders, H., "Concelebration," in *The Church and the Liturgy* (Concilium Series 2). Paulist Press, Glen Rock, N.J. 1964, 135-152.

McManus, Frederick R., "The Genius of the Roman Rite Revisited," *Worship* 54 (1980) 360-378.

Meagher, John, "Pictures at an Exhibition: Reflections on Exegesis and Theology," *Journal of the American Academy of Religion* 47 (1979) 3-20, especially 11.

Mitchell, Leonel L., *The Meaning of Ritual*. Paulist Press, New York 1977.

Mitchell, Nathan, *Cult and Controversy: The Worship of the Eucharist Outside Mass*. Pueblo Publishing Co., New York 1982.

Regan, Patrick, "The Fifty Days and the Fiftieth Day," *Worship* 55 (1981) 194-218.

Richstatter, Thomas, *Liturgical Law: New Spirit, New Style*. Franciscan Herald Press, Chicago 1977. Helpful study of the new liturgical legislation with clear chronological tables of its evolution.

Roles in the Liturgical Assembly (Papers of the 23rd Liturgical Conference Saint Serge), transl. Matthew J. O'Connell. Pueblo Publishing Co., New York 1981.

Saliers, Don E., "The Integrity of Sung Prayer," *Worship* 55 (1981) 290-303.

Schmemann, Alexander, *Introduction to Liturgical Theology*. American Orthodox Press, Portland, Maine 1966.

Scott, R. Taylor, "The Likelihood of Liturgy," *The Anglican Theological Review* 62 (1980) 103-120.

Seasoltz, R. Kevin, *New Liturgy, New Laws*. The Liturgical Press, Collegeville, Minnesota 1979. An excellent study of new liturgical legislation, with clear and extensive bibliographies.

Seasoltz, R. Kevin (ed.), *Living Bread, Saving Cup. Readings on the Eucharist*. The Liturgical Press, Collegeville, Minnesota 1982.

Strunk, William and E. B. White, *The Elements of Style*. Macmillan Company, New York 1959.

Symbol and Art in Worship. Eds. L. Maldonado, D. Power (Concilium Series 132). The Seabury Press, New York 1980.

Taft, Robert F., "The Structural Analysis of Liturgical Units: An Essay in Methodology," *Worship* 52 (1978) 314-329.

Taft, Robert F., "*Ex Oriente Lux?* Some Reflections on Eucharistic Concelebration," *Worship* 54 (1980) 308-325.

Taft, Robert F., "The Liturgical Year: Studies, Prospects, Reflections," *Worship* 55 (1981) 2-23.

Taft, Robert F., "Receiving Communion: A Forgotten Symbol?" *Worship* 57 (1983) 412-418.

Tegels, Aelred, "Liturgy and Culture: Adaptation or Symbiosis?" *Worship* 41 (1967) 364-372.

Turner, Victor, "Passages, Margins, and Poverty: Religious Symbols of Communitas," *Worship* 46 (1972) 390-412 and 482-494.

Turner, Victor, *The Ritual Process: Structure and Anti-Structure*. Aldine Publishing Company, Chicago 1969.

White, James F., *Introduction to Christian Worship*. Abingdon Press, Nashville 1980.